Ethics and the Modern Guru

Cults & Culture

Copyright © 2018 Ethics and the Modern Guru, a subsidiary of Thinking Agenda LLC

All rights reserved. This book or any portion thereof may not be reproduced or used in any manner whatsoever without the express written permission of the publisher except for the use of brief quotations in a book review.

The words of Melissa Deuter, Arno Michaelis, Pardeep Kaleka, Andrew Chesnut and Steven Van Neste remain their intellectual property and their rights remain to be identified as such, in accordance with the 1988 Copyright, Designs and Patents Act.

Cover art © Kyuin Shim.

For more information: www.guruethics.com

ISBN-13: 978-1985749696

Table of Contents

EDITORIAL

Every so often you hear it said: what a time it is to be alive. And of course, how could one not be impressed with all the progress and technological marvels that have given rise to the world we inhabit? There is, however, a downside to all this, as not just is this progress for the most part restricted to the Western First World, but we also tend to overstate this progress. What is meant by the latter, is that we are not as advanced a species as we like to believe, since our progress is always under attack of backwardness.

This backwardness is evidenced by the election of Donald Trump as the president of the United States of America, whose populizing slogan of "make America great again", is in effect not just a direct attack on progress, but also a deliberate stepping back from what has been achieved so far. Trump's tweetstorms may make great fodder for comedians, yet it must always be remembered his reign is a dangerous reality, not just because he won the presidency, but more importantly because a large amount of people allowed him said victory.

Much of the progress that has been achieved is due to a rather small amount of people. This is especially the case for all of our techno-scientific progress; we might like to think of modern man as technologically advanced, but this is a misnomer, as we merely are advanced consumers. We are familiar not with the microwave oven, but with its use, and much the same it is for ideas pertaining to society. Generally, as long as we are satisfied with our consumption, we won't think about it in a deeper sense. Similarly, when someone comes along and promises a greater consumption, we shan't blink an eye.

It really is no wonder how today's culture is one greatly dominated by the concept of the meme, as it is the ideal vehicle for thought-consumption. By itself, there is nothing wrong with the concept of the meme, however, the more it dominates, the greater becomes the chance of ignorance spreading. A lot could be written about memes, yet in reality they are mere advertisements of thought. What is peculiar about the way memes operate, however, is that they always come together with an element of satisfaction. In other words, when the meme is positively consumed, we imagine it is our thought as well.

The sharing of memes is like a sermon from the pulpit and with every like, one gets a new 'amen'. It ought to be obvious, that memes, combined with basic ignorance and the promise of 'greater consumption' is a recipe for disaster, hence the rise of cheap Populism and the victory of Donald Trump. One of the reasons people adore Trump, is because they find in him "someone who says it as it is". But what is meant by this? This, of course, is the way memes and Populism work, as its consumers buy into something they really don't know.

How does the slave know the master tells it as it is? This really lies at the heart of Populism and the social decay with which it goes hand in hand. It also comes to show, just how much we love the sound of the cracking whip, to the point we often don't even realize it is across our own back. Power not only corrupts but enthralls as well. As such, the allure of someone like Donald Trump (or populist leaders like him) is not just the cheap rhetoric, but the vision of power. Unable to think for ourselves, we fall prey to the cheap rhetoric of memes; unable to controls things ourselves, we fall prey to tough talking thugs.

It is easy to consume memes and cheap thoughts, yet at the end of the day, we always risk becoming the one being consumed. Of course, it is perhaps impossible to be free from prejudices, yet this should not mean one should not attempt. The problem is not just that there is an overall tendency to consume thought rather than to think, but that even outside the meme-sphere, we often are barraged by text which makes us feel as if we are thinking. This is the other element common to the rise of Populism: heated language that works on one's prejudices.

Selflessness may very well be a myth, yet this does not mean we should not always try and curb some of our selfishness. It is easy to think in terms conforming one's own bias, it is much harder to think in a way which considers the other. The way evolution works is through a process of never ending change and adaptation. Part of the beauty of evolution is its tendency to favor heterogeneity. The greater the variety of the gene pool, the greater the odds for a wide level of evolution.

Just as evolution thrives on otherness, so it is with thinking. The problem with Populism is, hence, akin to incest, and hence its rise can only lead to stagnation, maladaptation and death. Just as there is no such thing as a finished species, there will never be a finished society. Change is the inevitable constant, and the only way to successfully deal with it, is not by retreating in a bubble of self-same stagnation, but by daring to both think and move towards a different tomorrow.

STUCK IN THE SICK ROLE
AN INTRODUCTION TO
MELISSA DEUTER

As stated in the editorial, what a time it is to be alive, but of course not everything in the garden is rosy. The high-tech world in which we live may have simplified parts of life, but at the same time has added a new level of pressure and complexity. Next to the evolution of technology, there has also been an overall change in society, as there is an ever-increasing drive towards affluence.

The trend is that we no longer just want to be in the world, but want to make it in the world. Always the pressure is on to excel and be somebody, and this is not just the case among those born in upper- and middle-class families, but is common among poorer families as well. There is a constant need to do more than just survive in society, as what is desired is to be on top of it all. Due to everybody wanting to make it, the world has become a busy place, and often our minds are not ready to cope with it all, hence the topic of mental health has moved from the fringes to the center of society.

Just as we have become more health conscious, wanting to be at our physical best in order to cope with the world's demands, we now have also become more mind conscious. The oddity has occurred, however, that the more we become conscious of our mind, the more lost we feel in a world of stressful reality. Pressure is no longer for this or that person at the top, but has become for everyone, regardless of where they are. More importantly, pressure is no longer just for the employed salaryman, but has become a standard in the life of children, teens and adolescents.

Where in the past the field of psychiatry and mental health was mainly at the fringes, meant for the 'insane', today it has become more open. More importantly, a large part of mental health is now concerned with youth and adolescent development. Herein, however, lies a whole new problem, as we either rely too much on different forms of psychotherapy or too little.

Melissa Deuter's "Stuck in the Sick Role" is a breath of fresh air, as not only is she a legible and certified psychiatrist, but she also likes to walk a path that is rather different from the stereotypical pill-popping psychiatrist. The beauty of her work, is not just the absence of jargon, but the humaneness as well, and her drive to differentiate between mental disorders and ordinary moments of development.

Melissa Deuter – Stuck in the Sick Role – ISBN: 978-1937985769

One of the points of Deuter, is that indeed there is a slowdown in reaching adulthood, to quote the title of her opening chapter: "18 isn't 18 anymore". As evolution continues, it seems our period of reaching maturity is getting longer, perhaps not necessarily on a strict biological level, but rather on a deeper level of cognition. As mentioned before, we don't just want to be anyone, but want to be somebody; in other words, life is no longer just about filling the ordinary roles forced upon us through the dynamics of our upbringing and biology.

If, back in the days, kids left home at 18, then this was because the bio-societal complex was geared towards that, but the reason for this is that the world back then was a fair bit different, and lacked the complexity and diversity found in present day society. The world of today's adolescent is remarkably different from the past, not just because of the many technological advances, but also because the global access we have means that the world has become a place defined through speed. We live in a fast world, and perhaps this is why mental development comes to slow down, because our biology is not yet ready to deal with these immense velocities of present day society.

The strong point in Deuter's work is that she fully understands the complexity of modern society, yet also is wise enough to understand that a slowdown in reaching adulthood should not go together with a shirking of responsibility. As we became more conscious of mental health, there is this rising problematic, in which we start to identify too much with certain destructive moods and hence become stuck in mental illness.

Who are we? Who do we want to be? What once upon a time were questions asked exclusively by philosophers are now on the minds of almost every adolescent. It is also here another oddity presents itself, as we don't want to conform to society's direct wishes yet want to somehow reach the top of society at the same time. Rebellion, as such, is no longer this simple phase in which we assert our own taste, but rather turns into an elongated complex of self-discovery.

Melissa Deuter fully grasps the need for adolescent self-discovery, but at the same time she is weary as to how moments of ordinary confusion or anxiety can become misconstrued, and when not taken care of properly can lead to more serious issues of mental distress. Utmost care should always be given, to ensure we do not fall victim to identifying ourselves with mental conditions plaguing us. When we suffer from a cold we wish to overcome it, and our drive in overcoming the mental equivalent ought to be likewise.

In stark contrast to the overtly clinical approach, as found in those who reduce everything to brain chemistry, the work of Deuter is more of an anti-psychiatry, where the focus is on man and his environment. The aforementioned concept of responsibility is of vital importance here; our mental states may very well lead us to periods of distress, yet this does not absolve us from duty and responsibility.

What Deuter is opposed to, is the way whereby some surrender to their mental states and thus come to reinforce their symptoms. It is not that they are malingering, but rather that they have become despondent. It is interesting to note here, that what may be referred to as mental illness, is not a pathological something (the work of Thomas Szasz was pioneering here), but rather refers to highly subjective interpretations of how we feel inside.

Encountering a bothersome mental state is not the same as having a cold, for not only is there no pathogen involved, there also is no clear idea of what it means for that state to be gone. To illustrate, one may imagine an adolescent trying to find his career choice and find only confusion as to whom he wants to be. There is no clear idea of what it means to be free from that confusion, especially since often confusion arises out of a previous certainty.

The problem of a lot of mental healthcare is, however,

rather unfortunate, as it too much seeks to reduce everything to neural processes which it seeks to correct through psycho-pharmaceutics. Yet often this only reinforces the mental conflict, as the need for medication implies that I must be sick. The approach of Deuter, on the other hand, stresses structure and responsibility. Our focus should be on wanting to get better rather than on identifying with our distress.

For Deuter, getting on with life is instrumental to mental health, especially since the more we keep ourselves occupied the less our mind has a chance to wonder in the dark. It is alright for adolescents to slow down their development, but this does not mean the adolescent should be allowed to remain care free like a child. Rather, the adolescent should be steered to have a proper function and to contribute to the family.

The topic of communication is essential here. Parents should communicate to their child what is expected and provide proper motivation. Simultaneously, the parent should also allow the child to remain his own person. An important part of mental development is that we learn to form our own tastes and reasonings, and as a parent it is thus important we allow the child this freedom.

Mental health is precious, yet it often is hard to really pinpoint what it really entails. It is easy to feel anxious and confused in this busy world which often seems to be blowing itself to pieces, yet this does not mean we should surrender to forlornness. Instead, we should be brave and determined, to find our way through the many obstacles, and realize that happiness and fulfillment begins with us, through responsibility and determination.

AN INTERVIEW WITH
MELISSA DEUTER

Ethics and the Modern Guru:

Would you consider your work as a radically progressive approach, in helping to cope with emerging adulthood, and the stress and challenges presented by that?

Melissa Deuter:

No. I would actually consider my work as more of a "back to basics" approach. All psychiatrists are trained to look at the psychological development of our patients' problems in their environment. We know that life experiences shape many aspects of mental health.

Unfortunately, a lot of professionals discard what they learned about the importance of the environment in favor of a clinical focus on neuroscience-based and medication only treatment plans.

Ethics and the Modern Guru:

Given the sophistication of today's technologically driven times, do you think adolescents and young adults face different choices and challenges than they did in the past?

Melissa Deuter:

There is no doubt that today's youth face choices and challenges that are new. Social media is a source of new pressures, and even new forms of harm (cyberbullying). They must grapple with higher rates of pornography addiction and even things like sex trafficking risks. The world has changed quickly due to technology, and our kids are often in over their heads.

Ethics and the Modern Guru:
What guidance do you suggest for parents who feel they cannot get through to their teenagers, in trying to help them with topics such as bullying, peer pressure and undue influence?

Melissa Deuter:
Parenting is hard, and it's normal to struggle. But if things feel out of control, as for help—whether you talk to a friend or seek out the advice of a professional—I strongly advise parents to ask someone for support if they feel overwhelmed with what's going on with their kids.

Ethics and the Modern Guru:
What red flags should parents be aware of, that are not just part of the regular growing pains of being a teenager?

Melissa Deuter:
Teens and young adults who are in trouble often have a lot of trouble controlling their emotions. Maybe they cry at the drop of a hat, or they are angry all the time. Or even, they are scared to go to school. This is not new advice, but big changes in mood or behavior should be investigated by concerned parents.

Secrecy around internet usage is a newer red flag, and I

strongly advise parents to look over their kids' shoulders and know what they are doing online. If they are being sneaky, or if parents find evidence of something unhealthy via technology, it becomes important to restrict access and get advice from a professional.

Finally, teens and young adults need to have an open dialogue with their parents. If they stop talking, parents need to take notice and find out why.

Ethics and the Modern Guru:
How can parents be proactive in helping their adolescent children be motivated, especially when returning after having been on their own?

Melissa Deuter:
The best way for parents to get kids to take initiative is to make rules and hold them accountable. If you want them up and out of bed, getting things done around the house, make it a rule and require it.

Motivation is an internal quality. The best way to foster motivation is to create an environment of clear, solid expectations and follow through.

It also doesn't hurt to set a good example. Barking orders while you lounge on the couch doesn't work. Demonstrating the value of working toward your goals has a positive impact on kids' motivation.

Ethics and the Modern Guru:
What are reasonable expectations parents should have if their children return home?

Melissa Deuter:

If kids leave home to start adulthood, then fail or flop and come home, parents need to understand that they may lack experience with adult skills and behavior. Expectations and rules are reasonable but believing a 19-year-old with one failed college semester is going to come home and know how to act like a full-fledged grown up is unrealistic.

Still, it's okay to make rules and hold our kids to high standards. Parents can ask them to find a job, or enroll in community college, or both. Parents can ask them to get back to a structured, functional schedule promptly. In fact, parents should ask them to get up and function. Leaving them to wallow in their sense of failure won't help them.

Ethics and the Modern Guru:

Do you think kids being misdiagnosed leads to overmedication, and if so, on what scale do you think this occurs?

Melissa Deuter:

I think oversimplification leads to overmedication. If the doctor uses a simple checklist to diagnose depression or panic attacks, and never gets the back story, that's over-treatment waiting to happen. If a 20-year-old is sad and worried because she flunked out of college, or because her grandmother died, or because she just had a break-up, medication is probably not needed.

However, in our current world, doctors (and the public) tick off items from a checklist in the doctor's office, or on the internet, and diagnose depression while ignoring the back story. We want to blame the brain or genetics, and don't talk enough about life stressors and stages of development.

Overdiagnosis is an epidemic in mental health. Healthy people are talking too many psychoactive pharmaceuticals, while the seriously mentally ill cannot get the care they need.

Ethics and the Modern Guru:

You wrote about parents getting stuck with their kids in a setting enabling feelings of depression etc. As a parent how can you know you are enabling such feelings, and what can one do to become unstuck?

Melissa Deuter:

One of the things I note in the book is that doing the wrong thing usually feels wrong. Enabling is a very frustrating role for a parent. If you're enabling, you start to feel resentful and angry. Helping your kids in healthy ways is a very different experience. Truly helping feels good. I urge parents to listen to their intuitions if they find themselves growing resentful of the help they give to their kids. And then to get unstuck, stop doing the things that feel wrong. Say no. Set rules. Regroup and begin again with better boundaries.

Ethics and the Modern Guru:

With family structures changing, do you feel this has changed the dynamics on the parent-child relationship? For example, a very lonely elderly mom wanting to hang on to their kids to stay at home for company, support and protection?

Melissa Deuter:

Yes, I think some parents may be holding on to their kids.

But I'm not sure that is due to changes in family structure. For every aging mother holding on to her kids, there is another mom proudly pushing her kids to achieve their dreams, and then going off to her crafting circle to spend time with her own dear friends. The best way to become a healthy parent is to become healthy overall. Healthy parents make decisions that are best for kids, not to fill their own emotional voids.

Ethics and the Modern Guru:

How does one tell the difference between depression and defeat or despondency, and how does one know when to seek professional help?

Melissa Deuter:

Without training, it can be hard to know whether feelings of intense sadness represent normal life experiences, or they are something more. The best gauge is to ask yourself if feelings are a reasonable responsive to your circumstances, and if you are still able to cope with daily responsibilities. If you become unable to cope, and if that lasts for a long while, it might be time to ask a professional's opinion. But I don't advise seeing a prescribing professional first. Start with a talking professional, like a counselor or a therapist. Counseling professionals are highly trained and can make a recommendation for treatment if indicated. Most prescribing professionals will take out the prescription pad on the first visit, no matter what.

FROM HATE TO LOVE
INTRODUCTION

The great danger constantly lurking around the corner of an open society is that of vehement ignorance. Democracy stands as the rule of the people, yet this also means that Democracy can quickly falter and turn into a bubble of close-mindedness. Today's society is one marked by multi-culturalism, yet the more we come together, the greater is the force wherewith those opposed unite. This is evident in the sad rise of Populism in the Western First World, and the open cultivation of bigotry under the banner of freedom of speech and religious liberty.

From Trump to Brexit, the sad reality is not just a spreading of fear and ignorance, but also one whereby an identity is made out of it. The bigot never wants to admit to his hate, and hence dresses it in a royal robe. At the heart of today's Populism, there lies a need to picture one as victim who merely seeks to regain his lost status. In other words, the Populist acts like a prince who has lost his kingdom and seeks to reclaim it. This is evident in the figure of Donald Trump, whose populizing slogan "Make America Great Again" is a textbook example of this.

Of course, the blame does not lie solely with the Trumps of this world. The deeper problem always lies within the confines of our own skull, as the way ignorance spreads is through complacency rather than stupidity. It is always easy to blame things on people being stupid, but the fact is that smart people are capable of great stupidity as well. The problem, as such, is not so much one's level of intelligence, but rather one's level of emotional depth.

Emotional vulnerability is what is sought out by Populism, as it seeks to prey upon people's fears and concerns. At the heart of this, there always lies a drive towards a lost unity and a morbid fear of foreign influence. Ideas of law and order generally come together with Populism, as it seeks to impress through a play of power and discipline. Freedom, for the Populist, arises out of adherence to law, and the proper organization of a self-same culture. It is easy for the concept of freedom to become abused, and turned into a negative something, utilized to further bigotry. The best example of this is the rise of "religious liberty", where we find an active promotion of discrimination. The idea of religious liberty is not so much concerned with freedom, as rather it seeks to advance a specific ideological agenda and alienate those who are other.

Between religious liberty, Trumpian Populism and the conspiracy laden propaganda of false news sites such as Breitbart and Infowars, there is a dangerous rise of ignorance and bigotry. One thing all this has in common, is not just the hatred of everything that is other, but also a great uncertainty concerning one's own selfhood and identity. Another great problem, is that people caught in Populism etc. tend to overstate their own thinking.

The "fake news" hashtag may be famous because of Trump, but it has long been used by propaganda and conspiracy folks. All media is false, that is the general thought of the populist, everything is a conspiracy and we are here to liberate you. The idea they try to instill, is that we are trapped in media culture and hence do not think for ourselves, however, what they offer is not 'thinking' but just a low-level kind of feeling that fits within their tribalist ideology. The need for this sense of unity, is because the followers of Populism etc. tend to lack a coherent sense of self, and hence they can only feel authentic when they are in a world matching their own bias. This is also why bigotry tends to always come together with militancy, as it is a way of disguising the weakness of one's self. We hate the other because we lack the strength to be our own self, and thus we fall victim to confirmation bias presented through propaganda.

Whereas in Europe the problems of Populism and bigotry tend to not go much further than Islamophobia, in the United States of America there is still a much deeper culture of bigotry and racism. The fury with which the Trump regime is undoing everything president Obama built, goes far deeper than being merely political, as it is directly motivated by feelings of intense racism. What is even more problematic is the attempt to legitimatize hate speech, and under the banner of freedom of speech transform it as both regular and accepted. Freedom of speech is one thing, hate speech on the other hand is a whole different thing, hence the ignorance of proposed laws that institutions cannot refuse "controversial" speakers. Though everybody should always be free to say what he wants, it is never something that ought to be encouraged and legitimized to such a degree that it gives hate mongers a public platform.

The furore accompanying the decision of some cities to remove statues commemorating the Confederacy is a prime example of the emotional ignorance in which some dwell. Even worse, is how government officials, including president Trump, encourage such ignorance by defending such commemoration in the name of freedom and cultural heritage. But why would anyone want such a heritage? There lies a great sadness in the insistence of defending a heritage build solely on prejudice and enslavement. And the insistence of some to stand by their Southern heritage is not any different than if someone was to stand by Nazi culture. A heritage that is almost entirely based upon hatred and exclusion should never be celebrated, as it only serves to propagate cultural ignorance and deepen the wounds of those injured by said ignorance.

It is always important that we learn to look past slogans cheaply talking about freedom, likewise we should always be careful that our idea of freedom does not infringe upon that of others. The freedom promoted in the name of "religious liberty" is of a rather questionable nature, as it is solely based upon a negative. How can one talk about freedom, when its conceptualization is based solely upon discrimination? Perhaps the wise thing to do, would be to expand on our notion of freedom, and to allow ourselves the freedom to meet the other, rather than to banish or deport him. A person secure in his selfhood, should not be afraid to allow the presence of some other, and more importantly, one should never succumb to generalization and dehumanization.

A longing for sameness might very well be a part of all of

us, however, that does not mean we should always act upon it. It is one thing to want to be surrounded by likeminded people, it is a whole another thing to exclude all that is other. Perhaps it could be argued, that true freedom lies in the acceptance of the other, as it is through such acceptance one learns to stand on his own two legs.

The violence associated with White Supremacism, is evident not only of socio-cultural ignorance, but of a broken self as well; a self, incapable of functioning in a more evolved world. It is always helpful to be able to have a vision further than the length of one's own nose, hence we should always be mindful of small-minded rhetoric. It is easy to fall under the spell of hate groups and Populism, merely because one agrees to a point they make. A common element found in followers of White Nationalism and Religious Liberty is the attempt to soften and legitimize it, by saying they don't stand for hate, but merely are standing for their own rights. What they stand for, however, is "privilegism", the White Nationalist always sees himself as a class greater than every other.

Unconditional condemning of White Nationalism, Populism etc. is necessary, as we should never leave a backdoor for hate to enter our lives. We should always be vigilant and think critically, and allow for the presence of the other, just as we wish for the other to accept our own self. As a society we can only evolve by coming together and accepting each other's differences; hate and privilegism only lead to stagnation, and if we wish to grow, we must be daring to step in a borderless reality, allowing ourselves to be one and many at the same time.

AN INTERVIEW WITH
ARNO MICHAELIS

Ethics and the Modern Guru:

It's great to speak with you. With our publication, it's about having relationships with people, so it's not just about work, getting an interview and then goodbye, it's about learning, and as we do so, we develop further and evolve. And so, we're very particular about who we interview and who we establish connections with, because it's not mere business to us. We read your book and really enjoyed it, as we felt as if we were watching the movie of your life.

What really struck us was when you said the turning point was with raising your daughter, but we didn't see a lot of a step by step kind of approach to the whole process. We understood it, but remain pondering as well, as we imagine you did not just wake up one day and decided it was not going to be like this anymore. So, we are wondering if it was a kind of process of unlayering, with gradually things just falling off. Besides your daughter, were there any other issues that kind of snowballed into making you realize that perhaps you did not have a healthy viewpoint of humanity, and it would be better to steer clear of your ideology?

Arno Michaelis:

Yeah, it was a process. It—I use the word "exhausted" a lot in the last one—was certainly already in effect. The day I got in the white power skin head thing, and it built up over that period of seven years, until I finally went to leave. The exhaustion came from all sorts of directions. I

knew that what I was doing was wrong and yet did not have the courage to face that knowledge and to reconcile it. And so, I kept trying to suppress that knowledge, and that was exhausting. It was exhausting to cut myself off from the rest of the society, which you really must do in order to maintain that fragility of an ideology or vice versa. So, it was exhausting to not be able and enjoy the regular day to day cultural things, and as I mentioned in the book, it was most exhausting when people who I claimed to hate, treated me with kindness; when that happened, that indicated there was a shadow of a doubt, that perhaps my entire ideology was wrong.

I was wrong for following it. And yes, I did try to suppress that knowledge, and that is a lot of energy to constantly suppress. What I did, was to try and suck the hate out of me, eventually succeeding to the point where I started to think that maybe there's a better way to live my life. That maybe all these things that I'm so upset about and have me so wrapped up around them, are false. That maybe it is a waste of energy and I could be using it at better stops.

Ethics and the Modern Guru:
Do you feel like this is the case with most people that share those beliefs, or do you feel this was more unique with your situation? I mean, as you've encountered people that shared your belief, did you feel there are many different reasons, as to why people cling to racist ideologies?

Arno Michaelis:

I think anybody involved in a violent extremist mindset is exhausted. It sucks the life out of you. It's draining, and you're never replenished. It's a miserable way to live your life, and people who are in the throes of it will never admit it. If you can demonstrate a better way and help guide them to that, most people leave. It's just a matter of getting across, that there is a better way to live your life. So, when I work with people who are in hate groups, that is the angle I take, I say: "I lived your life for seven years. Everything you say and do, I bought that too". I tell them I was like that and that like me back then, they have not lived life. I tell them, how the life I lead now is with joy and gratitude, and that as I travel all over the world—everywhere I go—I am joyful to see all these other kinds of human beings, human beings that have way more in common with me than not. And instead of being terrified, if people seem different than me, I am fascinated by them, and attracted to them, as I see value in diversity. I have an active thirst for it now. And it's a far better way to live your life, than being terrified by everyone and everything at any given moment.

Ethics and the Modern Guru:

That truly is a great mission, though I imagine not without risks. Are the any dangers you have encountered? For instance, I imagine attempting to speak to a group of neo-Nazis, would be most dangerous.

Arno Michaelis:

Yes, I can't really go and speak to a group of them, as that would surely get me killed. I'm still a tough enough customer, but I'm pretty fragile from all the fights and have a lot of physical issues. If I went to a group of white supremacists they would beat the snot out of me, just as I would have done back then. The interactions I've had with people in the movement have been one on one. I am always mindful that hurt people hurt people, and I really believe that all violence in human history and all violence on earth, boils down to suffering that is not processed in a healthy way. And so, if I'm talking to someone who's hurting, and they latched onto these ideologies as a means of trying to address the trauma— however incorrectly—when I threaten that ideology, they will take that as a personal threat, a threat to their identity and who they are; therefore, the chance they will take a swing at me is always there.

Ethics and the Modern Guru:

So, when you approach, one to one, and they have these beliefs, how do you begin? Do you approach them with talking about your experiences, and start a dialogue out of this? It must be hard to get down to their level and hope they can find some connection with you, and then hope you can reign them in by the heartstrings and make them reflect upon their behavior. It seems like a delicate situation that takes a lot of skill and wisdom.

Arno Michaelis:

I think that under any circumstances—professionally or socially—you should always meet people where they are at. It is always good to not subject them to jumping through hoops; accept them for who they are, even when they say offensive things. It always is my approach to not butt heads on issues. I'm not going to debate whether or not Obama was coming to put them in a camp, or whether or not Donald Trump is good or bad. I'm going to talk to them as a human being, ask them how they feel and what personal things they have been through that led them to think the way they do.

I also emphasize the personal experience aspect of it all. I mean, such is the nature of social media. When I see inspirational stories on social media, I will be inspired and feel great. Or I may read about something that happened halfway around the world, something I am outraged about. Either way, my emotional response to the story affects the way I interact with the people who are right in front of me, as well as the way I live my life on a day to day basis. As such, I try to always challenge people to talk about what they have seen and experienced firsthand, rather than what you read about on the Internet.

Ethics and the Modern Guru:

That is very helpful, especially if we have some parents seeing their teenagers being influenced by harmful ideologies through social media. It is good advice, because too often, as a parent, you just want to grab your kids and scream at them, as like 'what the hell are you doing?' but that often is not the way to approach it.

Do you also speak in jails or prisons, or anything else of a similar nature?

Arno Michaelis:

I had a few talks throughout the county jail system; not many, but the few times were really rewarding, and I had some great conversations with the people going through the justice system.

Even though I was never incarcerated, I have been in jail quite a bit. I remember, that when I was a criminal, I feared and mistrusted law enforcement as sworn enemies to my ideology. I remember the days when I was driving around and when I would see a cop car, there would be this violent and visceral reaction inside of me.

Nowadays I am a good citizen and work with police officers quite a bit. It was all a matter of changing my perspective on things, rather than waiting for external things to change.

Ethics and the Modern Guru:

What do you think now of the sudden rise and marches of Neo-Nazi and White Nationalist groups? Not only does it seem on the rise, but at moments it seems to become publicly acceptable. There has been quite a bit of tragedy around it, as people try to counter the hate, but it sometimes appears to make things worse. What do you feel is the best and most proactive way in dealing with all of this, to let the hate dissolve rather than just fight everything head on, as this often leads to more death and tragedy?

Arno Michaelis:

I do believe, that as we progress as a society—and we learn and grow as a society the same way an individual does—that there will be growing pains. Based on what I have seen in my lifetime and by studying history, I think it is the kind of process that is two steps forward and then another backwards. People are afraid of change, and this instigates backlash against social progress, yet eventually as progress sets in, people who were making a big backlash come to realize there is nothing to be afraid of. Everything changes, and likewise we constantly keep moving forward this way.

A good example of that is how gay people are seen in our society today, which is vastly ahead of where it was twenty years ago, and even more so when compared to fifty years ago. And even though we still have progress to make, when my daughter was in high school, she had openly gay and transgender friends. It has been normalized to where kids and young people today no longer have a problem with one's sexuality, the way older people do. Similarly, I don't see race because there is just one race of human beings and we all are in it.

Today the idea of interracial marriage is a misnomer, it's not logically true. Whereas forty years ago, the idea of a black and white couple coming together in order to get married, would have been considered outlandish or even forbidden. Nowadays to kids it is just like second nature, and it's no longer a big deal. It shouldn't be! I have seen this happen in my own lifetime and have faith it will to continue as such.

The current resurgence of White Supremacist groups is certainly a cause for concern. There definitely is a backlash against the creeping social progress that has been taking place. That's inevitable, and I think that the best way to counter this, is by demonstrating that the fear behind it completely unfounded. If we organize an event that had people of all ethnicities, sexual orientations and religions come together to do something fun for the day, and we raised a bunch of money for a cause everyone can get behind, then we are actively demonstrating, that all the fears we may have about one another are absolutely unfounded.

You can be friends with gay people. You can be friends with Muslims, and they won't hit you with suicide bombs. People just like you want a good life to live; they want good things for their kids and they are not doing anything at anybody else's expense. The poverty mindset, that there is not enough, is completely unfounded. We can all live happy lives and thrive. If we just work together and care about one another, we can all live a decent life. We can all help each other thrive and live happily. The better off we all are, the better we are as a society.

Ethics and the Modern Guru:
You have started an organization to combat hate, what are its goals?

Arno Michaelis:
We founded "serve2unite" in response to the August 5, 2012, Sikh temple shooting, where a white power skin head—who was part of the gang that I had helped start in the late eighties—walked into a Sikh Temple and murdered six people. The Sikh community, within days of the shooting, decided they didn't want to just stand by, as this horrible atrocity had caused so much suffering. Instead, they wanted

to transform this atrocious hate crime into an inspiration for people to come together as one, and to grow together as human beings; driving towards a more peaceful society, where the kind of hate and violence that led to the shooting, would be less likely to happen.

I met Pardeep Kaleka who lost his father, Satwant Kaleka, in the shooting. Pardeep reached out to me, and asked me how this happened and how somebody could do this. My answer to that was practice. When you practice hate and violence, you become familiar with those things to the point where you not only become unfamiliar with love, peace, kindness and gentleness, but you also become repulsed by them. So, if you can imagine going through every waking moment of your life terrified by very person you see, you become violent; unfamiliar with the love you so desperately need, you become repulsed by it. You can get an idea of how someone's life becomes so miserable, that nothing but homicide followed by suicide seems to make sense.

So, when Pardeep and I had that discussion we also talked about our own lives, and I really wanted to know a lot about his dad. He told these stories about him and the more Pardeep and I talked, the more we had in common. Pardeep is a Punjabi man from the north of India, whose dad brought him to the United States with his mom and brother. Pardeep was six and his brother was four. They had nothing but perhaps $35 to name, and over a period of thirty years—

through almost superhuman dedication and devotion, work and love—they realized their American dream. Pardeep went from working in somebody else's gas station, to owning a bunch of his own gas stations and owning some rental properties. He now has a nice house in the suburbs, and has two adult sons, and some wonderful grandchildren. His sons graduated from Marquette and then right at the point where they realize the American dream, is when a miserably suffering skin head came in and murdered their grandfather and fellow Sikhs, saying they were not worthy of the American dream because they had brown skin and wore turbans.

In my case, I was born into the privilege of a Midwestern white kid. I literally had the American dream handed to me on a silver platter and spent most of my life trying to get away from it. I didn't want material things because I didn't want to be like all the kids I grew up with, and become a banker, lawyer or doctor, all that just repulsed me. And yet, as different as Pardeep and I may seem on paper, when we sat down to talk, we found out we had so much in common to the point where our dads acted alike as well as our daughters.

Our idea was to cultivate that, this beautiful truth that we have more in common than not, through a school program, and so we started working with middle school kids in two schools in Milwaukee, doing arts driven service learning and global engagement. We connect our students with really amazing superheroes, global mentors, who are located all around the world. A lot of them are former extremists like myself or survivors of violent extremism, and they all have amazing stories to tell and do amazing work. We would bring those people into our classrooms and they would inspire our young people and try to guide them in their service learning projects. Serve2unite has been doing this in schools since the spring of 13. We've worked in probably forty or fifty schools in the Wisconsin area and we've had face to face contact with tens of thousands of students.

Recently, Pardeep and I started working with small towns and communities going through demographic shifts. Where new group populations move in, existing populations become unsure and might feel threatened. We've worked with those little towns, to help everybody see that we can all get along together. We can all celebrate each other and work together to make life better for everyone. We are very honored to do this as an organization and want to really start aggressively expanding both nationwide and worldwide. We want to present our serve2unite program not only to schools, but to local communities as well, and get involved with local governments and community organizations. Both in the public and private sector, we want to really bring everyone together, and make them see we are all one human family, and the only thing stopping us from realizing this and celebrating it every day, is us.

Once we are determined to have faith in each other and have faith in humanity, then that humanity responds in kind and it reflects in the kind of society we live in. We're really looking forward to that step next year, and we're using the new book "The Gift of Our Wounds" as a kind of a springboard to do that. We really are appreciative that the more people who pre-order the book, all the more excited the publisher gets, and we want to sell as many copies in the focus that the more people who read it, the greater an impact we can have in society; to initiate healing processes, both individual and in essence, and to address the systemic issues. We really dedicate the book to all victims of violence throughout the world, and everyone who is suffering. We believe that the book is going to help initiate healing processes to affect the sea of changes in our society.

Ethics and the Modern Guru:
We believe it too. We are grateful for the opportunity to speak with you, thank you from all of us.

Arno Michaelis - My Life After Hate
(ISBN: 978-0983129097)

A former racist skinhead examines aspects of his past: Where did the hate begin? How did a teenage alcoholic become a central figure in the white power movement of the late 80s and early 90s? What happened to bring about his drastic change of mind and heart? With a collection of reflective essays, disturbing flashbacks, and an interview, My Life After Hate scrubs scabs off the festering wound of racism, then soothes with the essential wisdom of forgiveness and compassion.

"...a reckoning between who a person was and who a person can be. The drastic changes of Arno's perspective and the effects thereof clearly demonstrate that how we experience reality is up to us—that we can always choose compassion over aggression."—Bashir Malik, Artist, Milwaukee Community Elder

"Arno is a light in every room, filled with inspiration and hope, and knows the true articulation of forgiveness. Arno does a wonderful job of educating and exciting people around his message, as well as leading the cause against violent extremism."—Bailey Van Tassel, Founder, Abel Impact

"Arno is a truly exceptional public speaker and a man who demonstrates courage, sensitivity and compassion. If you are looking to engage young people, or indeed any people, in narratives of transformation and in understanding the mindset of violent extremism Arno will bring fresh insight and learning to this subject. Arno has shared his story with The Forgiveness Project for five years now and is one of our most engaging and effective speakers. I thoroughly recommend him."—Marina Cantacuzino, Founder/Director, The Forgiveness Project

"Arno is a living testament to the triumph of human bravery and goodness. Through his personal journey of hatred and prejudice to love and universal kindness, Arno has demonstrated in his committed effort to protect, nurture and guide the youths of today to be the next generation of leaders who are visionary, compassionate and brave."—Napa Chayaworakul, Meditation Instructor, University of Wisconsin Milwaukee, Communications Director, Milwaukee Shambhala Center

"It is my express pleasure to write in support of someone with whom I developed a friendship after having experienced his approach and excellent conduct in regards to anti violent extremism, harmony-building and peace-spreading. He is a true leader in this area of endeavour and I recommend him without hesitation as one of the best speakers you will ever hear from."—Mubin Shaikh MPICT, PhD (cand.), Consultant, National Security, Co-Author of Undercover Jihadi

"Arno has a unique way of articulating his story of coming from a background of negativity and growing into a champion of peace. His personal journey is very inspiring and provides those with hate in their hearts with a template for change."—Paul Carrillo, Executive Director, Southern California Crossroads

"We purchased Arno's book, My Life After Hate, for our collection. It was a hit with our readers, and touched many lives. I would recommend it to anyone interested in the topics of racism and personal healing."—Lisa Labovitch, Director of Library and Archives, Union League Club of Chicago

"Arno is an inspirational speaker and motivator. His personal story and commitment to social justice are important additions to the civil rights, human rights, and civil liberties advocacy world. He is an excellent coalition builder and partner in working for social change."—Hannah Rosenthal, CEO, Milwaukee Jewish Federation

"Reporters literally meet and interview thousands of people each year. Arno Michaelis stands out as one of the most honestly courageous people I've encountered. His fearlessness and message of hope, change and unity is not only eternal, but necessary right now when so many people are feeling such despair."—Suzanne Stratford, News Reporter, WJW-TV

"Arno is a passionate conduit and shining example of Positive Change. He has devoted his work to the betterment of others and for this he should be highly recognized as a great leader, advocate and inspiration."—Gill Hicks, Founding Director, M.A.D. for Peace

"Arno Michaelis is an insightful man whose life experience has garnered him a wealth of information that holds the key to unlocking the minds of racists of any color and successfully replacing the vitriolic hate through intelligent discourse. Hearing this man speak and watching him lead by example, motivates others to do their part to bring racial harmony to our society."—Daryl Davis, Owner, Lyrad Productions, Author of Klan-Destine Relationships

"Arno is an amazing speaker and his book My Life After Hate is a well written and important examination of the causes and consequences of hate and the capacity for people to change"—Peter Simi, Criminology Professor, University of Nebraska at Omaha

"Arno is an extraordinary individual whose exit from a life of hate has been an inspiration for so many trying to escape the prison of racism, violence and hatred. His autobiography My Life After Hate is essential reading for anyone attempting to understand the transformation of a former racist skinhead to a beacon of hope for others. Read his book, and if you're lucky, grab any opportunity you can to hear him speak."—John Horgan, Professor at the Global Studies Institute and Department of Psychology, at Georgia State University, Author of "The Psychology of Terrorism"

Invaluable Links:

https://serve2unite.org
https://medium.com/@arnomichaelisIV

AUTOBIOGRAPHICAL NARRATIVE STATEMENT
by Pardeep Kaleka

Trauma therapist and Co-founder of Serve2Unite (S2U), which is an organization that was founded in response to the Sikh Temple tragedy in Oak Creek, Wisconsin on August 5, 2012. During this tragedy I lost my father, Satwant Singh Kaleka, and nearly lost my mother, Satpal Kaur Kaleka, both of whom were inside the Temple that Sunday morning. The shooter in this attack was a "White Supremacist", Wade Michael Page, whose primary motivation was ideology and hatred. This atrocity was the worst single race-based attack that our country had seen in fifty years. Since the 16th Street Baptist Church bombing in Montgomery, Alabama, which took the lives of four very precious little girls who were finishing up service that day. Both of these shootings were carried out by "white supremacist" organizations, in 1963 by the KKK and in 2012 by The Hammerskin Nation. While the 1963 bombing was tragic, it was the catalyst that inspired so much progress, and we felt that the shooting at the Temple should also inspire that kind of movement. So following the shooting, we as a community saw the importance of responding to the tragedy, and hatred with kindness and compassion, not only to heal but also to raise awareness of who we are and what we represent to this "American Dream". My family, which includes my younger brother, Amardeep, my mother Satpal and my father Satwant, was your typical first-generation immigrant family. We originally came from a region of Northeast India, called Punjab. This region is located near the border of neighboring Pakistan. To say that India and Pakistan have been embroiled in conflict would be a very gross understatement. This embattlement of regions has as much to do with politics, as it does with religion and land. However, for these reasons as well as economic reasons, my family migrated to the United States in 1982.

My family settled in South-Eastern Wisconsin, where we lived the typical "Immigrant Dream", which I also call the typical "American Dream", in the realization that America was originally built on the sacrifices of so many immigrants that came before us. Traditionally in India my family was a farming family, however here in the city of Milwaukee, farming was not really an option. I remember that times were very hard and both my mom and dad took on odd jobs to make ends meet. We had a very small community, as there were not very many Sikh families who had migrated to the Midwest at that time. Although the Sikh community was small, our community was very close. I remember fond times of staying with family members to get by simply because we did not have much. This was our life until my father took a leap of faith to buy a small full-service gas station on the south-side of Milwaukee. The entire family worked here and this store was truly your typical "mom and pop shop". Throughout these experiences my family became a staple in the south side community and my family achieved success. My first job, as I was 11, was to pump gas, check tires and clean windows at our full-service gas station. It was here that I was first exposed to customer service, and learned invaluable lessons on the psyche of what makes people click. Ultimately as most of the convenience stores in Milwaukee started to convert from full-service to self-service, my father thought it would be best for us to follow this trend. Through good fortune my parents became successful entrepreneurs, and my brother and I could concentrate on our education, thus allowing us to both graduate from Marquette University. My father had truly achieved his American Dream, this was until he was murdered by a White Supremacist on August 5, 2012 who wrongly believed that immigrants are not entitled to this fundamental "pursuit of happiness" that our forefathers had built this great nation upon.

For ten years I taught "at-risk" High School youths in the city of Milwaukee, and formerly for five years I served as a police officer in this same neighborhood, commonly referred to as 53206. In both of these capacities, it became clear the role that limited exposure and the cycle of violence plays on our community. Numerous times I have observed that youth and adults only know one way of life, and unfortunately, this is often one that involves violence. Shortly after the shooting on

August 5, we formerly founded a non-profit called Serve2Unite that encourages communities to address these cycles of violence and become agents of change, who work on various areas for the "Social Wellness" of all. S2U's vision is to use service work, global engagement, and artistic expression to address issues that exist in our communities. We focus on the theme that "common goals relating to service work, magnify commonalities of humanity, thus creating stronger community bonds". In this process we understand that forgiveness is necessary. However, forgiveness was eluding our own community because there were so many details and "whys" related to this incident that were not answered. The shooter, Wade-Page had killed himself shortly after he took the lives of six others, your typical murder-suicide. To find answers I reached out to the only person who I thought could provide me with this understanding of why, Arno Michaelis. The reason Arno could provide me with understanding of this, is because for eight years of his life Arno was also a white supremacist, Arno had also been a recruiter, Arno was a lead singer of a hate metal band, and Arno was a founding member of The Hammerskin Nation. All of these commonalities he shared with Wade-Page, so I felt he was the only one who could provide me with some answers of why. Honestly speaking, I also envisioned some kind of apologetic response from him, seeing that he was instrumental in bringing the "movement" to South-Eastern Wisconsin-Milwaukee region. However, from the moment we sat down, we discovered the truth that the more you understand about someone, the harder it is to hate them, even if they have committed some very unspeakable acts. Today, Arno and I share our story of transformation, and forgiveness to audiences all over, with the work we do for Serve2Unite. For me personally, he has become a mentor and brother, and for our community he has become a true ally.

One of Serve2Unite's most successful programs is the school program in which we have partnered up with Arts @ Large to create student leadership chapters of S2U in schools. These students from different schools are involved in numerous service projects in and out of their communities. Students conduct research, provide answers, celebrate each other and post their creative responses for peace and nonviolence to a global audience. Also contributing to the work of our organization are peace activists, former-violent extremists, former-survivors, educators, and parents. Some of the partner agencies are: Against Violent Extremism, The Forgiveness Project, Over My Shoulder Foundation, and Formers Anonymous. This collaboration helps students see their work globally, thus taking their responsibility for their community seriously, and cementing the importance of values such as diversity, kindness, compassion, forgiveness, and positive perceptions. Our mission is to make the practice of peace an attractive and valuable way of life for students, thus transforming not only just their school environment but also being social agents of wellness for the entire community. The work of our students, and global mentors can be found on our online www.serve2unite.org. We have facilitated with nearly 20,000 youth in the past 4 years, and currently we are working with numerous schools within the Milwaukee Community to address trauma and healing. Over the past year, I have been working as a therapist to assist survivors of sexual trauma in their healing journey. We find that if we want to successfully address trauma, we must put the proper foundation in place for survivors to be successful. This often time looks like the Restorative Model of repairing harm, and understanding rather than our society's preoccupation of punishment, comparison, and judgement.

I whole-heartedly believe that the community, our faith, and the intrinsic purpose to heal has propelled us into the mission that we embark on today. While I would love to say this happens by accident or maybe happenstance, I know better. I know that we must take deliberate action moving forward. Each situation, circumstance, and tragedy is an opportunity as well as an obstacle. We, with humanity, have the ability to define each situation, circumstance, and tragedy. In conclusion, if and only if, we are able to shed light from darkness, turn tragedy into triumph, or give birth from the ashes will we be able to keep future generations safe. If we become miserable from the acts of hatred, then hatred has won and we will continue the vicious cycle.

SANTA MUERTE
INTRODUCTION

Perhaps one of the most beautiful aspects of multi-culturalism is that it serves as a kind of living present day anthropology. There is, however, always a problem when it comes to anthropology, namely the bias of one's own culture. It is always tempting to see other cultures as inferior, yet in reality, different cultures have always more in common than not. An instrumental figure here was Claude Lévi-Strauss, who opposed the idea of the savage mind being different from the civilized mind, and instead said there is only one human mind. With this in mind, we may argue, that in reality there is only one society, and that cultural clashes tend to be paradigmatic, rather than being rooted in actual differences.

What is true for anthropology is true for religious study as well, and it is important to keep this in mind, since multi-culturalism often comes together with a clashing of different religions. Such clashes were especially common in the days of European conquest, when Christianity was as its height of forcing itself upon the "savage nations" conquered, and European society posited itself as the one true civilization. The arrival of the slave trade furthermore complicated the intensity of cultural clashing, and gave rise to the formation of new religions, as now people found themselves in an alien world.

The slave trade added fuel to the fire, because beside the obvious reasons of physical oppression etc., slaves had the dominant religion forced upon them, and at the same time they also had to deal with the remnants of indigenous religion. The fascinating oddity here, is that all this turmoil and oppression makes a rather fertilizing soil in which new religious thought may come to grow, and though such new traditions, tend to be seen as simple folk faith, they often have a rather incredible level of ingenuity.

To most, folk faiths in the American continent will appear as a mixture of supernatural mumbo jumbo and vile beliefs, though of course, this just comes to show the workings of prejudiced minds. The sad reality is that too often these folk faiths only come to stand in our awareness through negative press. The word Voodoo is, to many, synonymous with outdated beliefs involving sacrifice and endangerment, and usually we only hear about it whenever something goes wrong, as in cheaply screaming headlines in the nature of "person killed during Voodoo exorcism ceremony". In reality, however, many folk faiths are not any more 'backward" than the regularly accepted mainstream faiths, and the people condemning folk faith, often forget the absurdities present in their own faith.

Perhaps more importantly, people tend to be too quick to dismiss folk faiths as being primitive, and hence fail to see their cultural significance, as well as their hidden intelligence. As it is notorious just because of its name alone, Voodoo is a perhaps the best example. Wes Craven's "The Serpent and the Rainbow" might have fueled our imagination, but the book upon which it is based, written by the anthropologist Wade Davis, paints a rather soberer picture. The beauty of Davis' work is that it showed a historical perspective, and illustrated how Vodou grew out of the Haitian slave revolt, and continues to be a part of deeper layer of Haitian society.

Vodou, the genuine religion rather than the thrilling term voodoo, came to be as slaves tried to cope with a new world, and regain their freedom. The end result, is an amalgamation of Catholicism, the native faiths of the salves, and whatever remained of the echoes of Hispaniola's native Taino faith. As such, rather than a cheap superstitious faith, Vodou is an intricate faith, which stands outside the regular evolution of religion, as it's driving force is one of a displaced people trying to form new roots.

Though being the most popular by name, Vodou is just one of a multitude of folk faiths in the Americas, most of which still thrive in spite of negative press. In the city of Orlando, for instance, it is not at all uncommon to stumble across little stores called Botanicas, which generally are associated with Santeria, and carry a variety of religious supplies. Rather than being some primitive fringe thing, these folk faiths are every bit as established as the regular accepted faiths.

Though Christian dominance enjoys placing folk faith in a bad light and tends to place it in the category of devil worship, this only reveals how intimidated established faith is by it all. The irony is, however, that looking at it historically, Christianity became dominant by using elements of established pagan faiths; as such, it may be argued that—aside dogma—the path of folk faiths often bears a striking resemblance to early Christian history. One of the elements of early Christian history that makes folk faith so attractive, is that there is much less of a focus on a central dogmatic authority, and hence everything relies more on immediate connections.

Whereas established faith tends to be metaphysical in nature, folk faith often is more rooted in the directness of society, so the irony is, that in in spite of its 'primitive' appearance, it tends to be more focused on reality than established faith, and it is this which brings us to the figure of Santa Muerte.

Steven Van Neste – Santa Muerte 3 – oil on canvas

As touched upon already, folk faiths tend to become notorious due to negative press, and the cult of Santa Muerte is no different here, and yet in spite of her ill repute, her worship is said to be one of the fastest rising religious movements. One thing that ought to be noted before anything else, is that the word "cult" here, is used in the context of "adoration", rather than in the sense of a closed nefarious group.

The best way to describe Santa Muerte is as a female grim reaper, yet in all irony her worship is much more centered around life, than it is around death. Her infamy is, however, not so much due to her grim reaper form, as it is mainly due to her connection with crime and the Mexican drug cartels. The association with crime is enough for most to envision her as something satanic, yet in reality this is not a primary connection, as the primary focus of Santa Muerte, is more in line with that of a patron saint of the poor, the hopeless and the downtrodden.

As tends the be the case, the rise of Santa Muerte goes hand in hand with societal changes, and hence, if she encroaches upon established faiths, then this is mainly because they fail to address the immediate needs of those deciding upon following Santa Muerte. Established faiths' focus tends to be metaphysical in nature and is centered around eschatological themes, as such, their consolation always lies in the afterlife, and they see in living a burden to be borne. In established faith, the divine lies outside of man, and though one may pray for something, one always remains at the mercy of God's will and grace. Santa Muerte, on the other hand, presents herself as more of an active force ready to interfere and provide here and now.

As mentioned already, in spite of Santa Muerte being a female grim reaper, she otherwise has no direct connection to the realm of the death. Perhaps one could say, that her agency is that of those living in the shadow of death, as she generally is seen as a protector of the outcast. In part, the strength of Santa Muerte is that all are equal in death; rich and poor not only die the same, but in skeletal form cannot be differentiated from one another.

Santa Muerte statue with candle

Notorious as she may be due to her association with crime it would be unfair to portray her as a criminal deity, as rather this connection seems to be due to poverty forcing one into crime. Due to her imagery's connection with the Mexican drug cartels (popularized, for instance, in the crime drama "Breaking Bad"), it is obviously tempting to see her as a demonic entity hellbent on evil, yet this is not so. As ominous as she may appear, Santa Muerte should never be seen be seen as some supernatural hitman, as her association is with justice rather than atrocity.

The other part of Santa Muerte's notoriety, is due to the swift animosity of the Catholic Church. It is of course to be expected that mainstream Christianity is opposed to both Santa Muerte and folk faith in general, as it always seeks to dominate. Protestant faiths in general, have always been more opposed to anything "pagan", something especially true in the often fundamentalist incarnations of American Protestantism. Due to its variety of saints and mystics, Catholicism has always maintained somewhat of an esoteric nature, this is especially the case in Latin America which, besides being the richest territory in folk saints, also tends to have the greatest number of Catholics. The Catholic Church may very well always distance itself from folk faith elements, yet the condemnation it has given to Santa Muerte is much harsher than anything bestowed on other such figures and beliefs.

As tends to be the case with such topics, it is rather hard to separate the wheat from the chaff, for not only is there a bias against Santa Muerte, but there is also a market of people using Santa Muerte for commercial purposes. Folk faith often is a complicated thing to study, not because there is a shortage of believers, but rather because it is hard to come to an objective view, rather than being swayed by mere hearsay and sensationalism.

Enter then Andrew Chesnut, who is a professor of religious studies at the Virginia Commonwealth University and specializes in Catholicism and the traditions of Latin

Andrew Chesnut – Devoted to Death – ISBN: 978-0199764655

American folk faiths. His latest book is entitled "Devoted to Death" and deals exclusively with the skeleton saint known as Santa Muerte. Not only is Chesnut an expert in the spiritual traditions of Latin America, he also has a genuine enthrallment with it all, combined with an unbridled passion, to present everything as lively as possible.

Having interviewed a great multitude of Santa Muerte devotees—both north and south of the border—Chesnut's book reveals an intricate view of the Bony Lady in all her glory and facets. The strength of his work is his focus on all aspects of Santa Muerte, and all of this is presented in manner that is both scholarly and friendly. Best of all, there is an openness to his work, allowing the reader to come face to face with Santa Muerte, in a landscape of fascination rather than condemnation. Most beautifully, he also describes how it is unfair to see her as a patroness of criminals, as she is honored on both sides of the law, since even policemen will seek her favor and protection.

Of course, the connection with crime is only one aspect of Santa Muerte, and Chesnut does well in dispelling the myth that she is just some supernatural hitman. To many, as such, it might come as a surprise that she is also highly regarded in matters of love and healing; concerning the latter, Santa Muerte also aids in overcoming one's problems with addiction. The beauty of Santa Muerte is, that she is willing to listen to anybody and aid that person as needed; so far from being a satanic agent, she is presented with kindness and understanding.

AN INTERVIEW WITH
ANDREW CHESNUT

Ethics and the Modern Guru:

At one point there was this turning in your career, where you moved away from research into the Virgin of Guadalupe, and instead came to focus on Santa Muerte. Having done so much research, is it still the same passion, or do you feel you have come full circle with it?

Andrew Chesnut:

Yes, Santa Muerte is interminably intriguing, with so many different facets to consider, so I feel just as passionate about the research on her as I did when I started nine years ago. Since I began my research not long after her cult went public in 2001, I've been fortunate to have a front row seat to the drama of devotion to her becoming the fastest growing new religious movement in the Americas.

Ethics and the Modern Guru:

It often seems Santa Muerte just appeared out of nowhere, what would you consider are her genuine origins?

Andrew Chesnut:

That's because until 2001 she was venerated clandestinely as a figure of the occult. Mexico is home to the world's second largest Catholic population on earth, after Brazil, so historically folk saints, other religious practices and sorcery had to be conducted clandestinely. The Mexican folk saint of death is the result of syncretism between the Spanish Grim Reapress (la Parca) and indigenous beliefs in death deities. As part of the conquest and colonization of Mexico and most of the Americas, the Spanish Catholic Church brought with it the Grim Reapress as a tool of evangelization of the indigenous populations. The Spanish had no idea that many indigenous groups, such as the Aztecs and Mayans, had complex religions which included death deities, such as the Aztec goddess, Mictecacihuatl. Some indigenous groups in central Mexico interpreted the Grim Reapress through their own religious lens and turned la Parca into a supernatural miracle-worker, Santa Muerte. It should be noted that in Spain la Parca was a mere personification of death without supernatural powers.

Ethics and the Modern Guru:
Is there a common denominator among the many different types of devotees?

Andrew Chesnut:
With an estimated 10 million followers, there are devotees from all walks of life, including doctors, lawyers, and Mexican government officials. However, in Mexico and Central America her devotional base is largely younger urban dwellers without much formal education. Since there has been no systematic large-scale survey of devotees, I base my assessment on a decade of research. As a death saint she naturally has a special appeal to those who feel like their demise might be just around the corner, thus narcos and others who are exposed to violent death find her especially

appealing for both purposes of protection and harm to others. Since death never discriminates, she's also very popular among LGBTQ folks and has even become an unofficial patron saint for many with alternative sexual identities in Central and North America.

Ethics and the Modern Guru:

We know that the Catholic Church is highly opposed to Santa Muerte, of course, they generally are against folk saints, but the vehemence against Santa Muerte seems to be more intense. Do you think they consider her to be some sort of a devil?

Andrew Chesnut:

Yes, the Catholic Church and many Protestant denominations view the skeleton saint as satanic. In standard Christian theology death is viewed as the last enemy of the eternal life that Jesus offers to believers through his ultimate sacrifice on the cross. To venerate death is to negate the promise of eternal life. There are alternative Catholic views from the Medieval era which view death as a gentle sister, but these have been overshadowed by the now hegemonic view in the Church that the female death saint is evil and must be combatted.

Ethics and the Modern Guru:

There is no shortage of folk saints, yet Santa Muerte seems to stand out more than others, and even tends to cross over into the practices of other folk spirituality. What do you think is the uniqueness she possesses to cause this?

Andrew Chesnut:

Santa Muerte statue in Nuevo Laredo

She's the only female folk saint of death in the Americas. The two other skeleton saints, Rey Pascual from Guatemala, and San la Muerte from Paraguay and Argentina, are very similar but are male figures. Her meteoric growth mostly owes to her reputation as the speediest and most efficacious miracle-worker on the Mexican and Central American religious landscapes. Working-class devotees tend to be very pragmatic in their petitions to her, and millions believe that she's the one who comes through the quickest and most often on miracles relating to health, wealth, and love.

Ethics and the Modern Guru:

The rise of Santa Muerte is described as one of the fastest growing "cults", is this mainly among Latinos, or do you see it spreading beyond?

Andrew Chesnut:

I prefer to classify it as new religious movement since the term "cult" often lends itself to confusion and means one thing among academics and quite another in popular usage. I'd estimate some 95% of devotees are of Latin American origin. However, devotion to her is also fast growing among Euro-Americans and Afro-Americans. There are at least ten English-speaking Facebook groups for devotees. Interestingly, most of these devotees seem to be LGBTQ. Beyond North and Central America, there are now devotees in South America, Europe, the Philippines, India, Japan, South Africa, New Zealand, and Australia!

Ethics and the Modern Guru:
The imagery of Santa Muerte is, at first glance, rather intimidating, so how is it that she is so associated with healing?

Andrew Chesnut:
Excellent question! Death as a healer has antecedents in European, especially German folklore. If death can extinguish life, then who better to petition for a few more grains of sand in her hourglass of life? Since skeletons and skulls and Day of the Dead are an integral part of Mexican culture, many don't view her skeletal visage as intimidating or frightening. Her role as curandera or healer is of paramount importance but completely obscured in media portrayals of the Skinny Lady (la Flaquita, one of her common monikers).

Ethics and the Modern Guru:
The greatest infamy of Santa Muerte is her relation to the Mexican cartels. Has there always been this connection between her and crime, or is this something that came later?

Andrew Chesnut:
Her connection to organized crime in Mexico first came to light in the late 1980s. Most infamously Cuban narco Adolfo was practicing an aberrant form of the Afro-Cuban religion Palo Mayombe on a ranch in northern Mexico. Santa Muerte images were found at the compound where some sixteen

people, including a University of Texas student, had been murdered as part of ritual sacrifices. It's unclear what role the skeleton saint played in his "narcosatanism," but it was the first time Santa Muerte was featured in the press as a supernatural figure linked to organized crime. Since then she has carved out a strong following among narcos. Given her purported ability to cause and prevent death she's a natural choice for cartel members seeking supernatural power to carry out their business. She also has a robust following among Mexican law enforcement, especially municipal police, so she's really more of a patroness of the narco wars than exclusively a saint for narcos. Just last month I discovered that there's at least one American devotee of death among federal law enforcement here in the U.S.!

Ethics and the Modern Guru:

Santa Muerte is associated with both speedy justice and criminality, as such, is there a larger connection between these two elements, as it involves Her? Also, are there instance of criminals devoted to Santa Muerte who change their ways, or perhaps even of corrupt people within the "justice department" changing their views?

Andrew Chesnut:

She's the patroness of the entire Mexican penal system with a robust following among not only inmates but also prison guards, social workers, and law enforcement. The green colored Santa Muerte of law and justice serves as a supernatural advocate arguing for the best deal for her clients, such as speedy release from prison. One of my nephews in Michoacan used to be a prison guard at the state penitentiary in Morelia and told me that she's by far the most popular saint among inmates there and that about one quarter of his fellow guards are devotees. The Bony Lady (la Huesuda, another popular sobriquet) is also increasingly popular in U.S. prisons, especially in California, Texas, and the Southwest. In fact, I was recently asked to give a talk on Santa Muerte to American prison chaplains at the annual conference of the American Academy of Religion. I'm not aware of inmates who've had a conversion experience via devotion to Santa Muerte, but it's not hard to imagine that scenario.

Ethics and the Modern Guru:

It seems that Santa Muerte is someone who reveals deeper fears and wishes without any added judgement. When you were interviewing devotees, were there stories of how inner conflicts got resolved?

Andrew Chesnut:

Santa Muerte votive candles
(photographer: T. Carter Ross)

No, Santa Muerte is more about dealing with the hardships of poverty, violence, sickness, and romance, so devotees tend to be more focused on solutions to pressing problems of survival as opposed to moral dilemmas and psychological issues.

Ethics and the Modern Guru:

Are there instances of people devoted to Santa Muerte, who otherwise did not fit within a paradigm of Catholic based spirituality?

Andrew Chesnut:

Yes, most African-American and Euro-American devotees approach Saint Death more within a NeoPagan or Magick paradigm. There is one great exception, however, Steven Bragg, the devotional pioneer in New Orleans, leads veneration of her in accord with her Mexican folk Catholic heritage. Both in Mexico and the U.S. Santa Muerte is increasingly cross-fertilizing with Afro-Cuban Santeria to the extent that the great Santa Muerte devotional pioneer, Enriqueta Romero of Tepito in Mexico City, has an entire room in her home reserved for Santeria paraphernalia.

Ethics and the Modern Guru:

What are the origins of the rituals and magic associated with Santa Muerte? It seems similar to other instances of folk magic, are the workings of Santa Muerte associated with this?

Andrew Chesnut:

There are diverse historical influences, but most importantly Spanish and indigenous practices of sorcery and magic. Even though Spain was one of the most Catholic nations on earth at the time of the conquest of the Americas, pagan practices, such as love magic, survived and were brought to the New World. Indeed, Santa Muerte love sorcery is entirely Mediterranean in origin. The only novelty is the skeleton saint herself. More recent influences are New Age, which is huge in Mexico, NeoPaganism, and Santeria. Since there is no official church of Santa Muerte, new influences are absorbed like a sponge.

Ethics and the Modern Guru:
Are there other folk saints similar to Santa Muerte?

Andrew Chesnut:
Except for their male identities, death saints Rey Pascual and San la Muerte are practically identical. Their iconography derives from the male Grim Reaper, and the types of petitions and rituals are close kin to those of their female cousin. Interestingly in Guatemala, Santa Muerte now appears to be more popular than native Rey Pascual, perhaps in a case of Mexican religious imperialism. Mayan shamans whom I interviewed a few years ago at Rey Pascual's temple in the town of Olintepeque, were working with both him and Santa Muerte, and one characterized them as spouses. Curiously, the Church has specifically rebuked Santa Muerte but not her male counterparts, recalling that Pope Francis is Argentine and certainly is familiar with San la Muerte.

Ethics and the Modern Guru:
The current popularity of Santa Muerte, has this been achieved through a slow growth over time, or have there been specific historical situations accelerating her fame.

Andrew Chesnut:
The lion's share of meteoric growth has occurred only in the past fifteen years since her cult went public in Tepito. So unknown was Santa Muerte to the great majority of Mexicans prior to 2002 that my parents-in-law, who have lived their entire eighty-seven years in the state of Michoacan, only found out about the skeleton saint through my research!

Now it would be almost impossible to find a Mexican who hasn't heard of the Pretty Girl (la Nina Bonita, another common nickname).

Ethics and the Modern Guru:

Finally, is there a connection between Santa Muerte and ancestor veneration?

Andrew Chesnut:

There doesn't appear to be one historically, but many devotees are now integrating ancestor veneration into their practice. At this point the most significant example of it is the incorporation of Santa Muerte into day of the dead rituals by many devotees. In fact, it's become such a common practice in Mexico, that for the past five years or so, the Church in Mexico issues warnings against bringing the skeleton saint to the cemeteries or putting her on home altars. And for the first time ever the Catholic press in the U.S. issued the same warning in the days prior to November 2, 2017.

Santa Muerte statues for sale among others (photographer: Andreas Praefcke)

WHAT'S WHAT & WHO'S WHO

The world of American folk faith is fascinating and large, and it can fill many books. It is a bewildering topic, yet we felt like at least adding a few notes to show its dazzling beauty.

First of there are quite a few different religions, to the novice they may all seem the same, but in reality, they all have their own uniqueness. What they often do have in common, is three elements; the African continent, the slave trade and the influence of local culture. The impact of slave trade is usually at the hands of Spanish conquistadores, though it also happened at the hands of the French, as is the case with Haitian Vodou.

Due to negative press and its use in entertainment, the term 'voodoo' is very well known, and hence also tends to be the most abused. When it comes to the real Vodou, what must be understood is that there are different forms, which are only loosely connected.

The main place of Vodou is the island of Hispaniola, which houses two countries, Haiti and the Dominican Republic, which each have their own separate form of Vodou. Haitian Vodou grew out of the French slave trade and ties in with the Haitian slave revolution. It is a complicated system, mainly dominated by three classes of spirits, namely the more settled Rada, the fiery and revolutionary Petro and the ever popular Gede, who are associated with death and the graveyard, and whose most popular one is Baron Samedi. The name given to spirits is Lwa, which is a Haitian Creole term meaning law (from the French "lois"). Dominican Vudú (las 21 Divisiones), by contrast, grew out of the Spanish slave trade, and is considered looser than Haitian Vodou. The two share many similar spirits, but their syncretizations may be different.

Syncretization is something most common in folk faith. As slaves were forcibly converted to Christianity, they used Christians saints to retain their own faith. Syncretization can also be seen as instrumental in furthering the magic that comes together with folk faith, as even in Europe there always was an 'underground' of magical operations using saints. With this in mind, it also ought to be noted, that the term brujeria does not denote a folk faith as such, but simply means witchcraft, the term curandero likewise means healer. A lot of magical practices in folk faith can be traced back to witchcraft and occultism in Europe.

Furthermore, though there are resemblances with Haitian Vodou, New Orleans Voodoo is different. Louisiana Voodoo grew independently of Haitian Vodou, though during the revolutionary wars, there were Haitian troops fighting the British, as such there is at least somewhat of a connection between the two. New Orleans Voodoo is often more based upon the old world, and lacks the more revolutionary aspects as found in Haitian Vodou. It also ought to be noted, that New Orleans Voodoo has a much greater emphasis on magic. The notorious voodoo doll, for instance, is mainly a New Orleans Voodoo thing. Hoodoo is a further development of

New Orleans Voodoo, in which almost all religion has been stripped and what remains is magic. Also, whereas New Orleans Voodoo is Catholic in nature, Hoodoo tends to be more associated with the Protestantism of Southern USA.

Generally, most Vodou grew out of the culture of slaves brought from Western Africa, specifically the Fon, Ewe and Kabye people, though Haitian Vodou also has a lot more influence from the deeper regions of Central Africa, especially Congo. Vodun, as such, also exists as the traditional religion of these people, though this religion is separate from the faiths and practices that grew out of it. Other faiths that grew out of it are the Cuban Vodú (la Regla de Arará) and the Jejé aspect of Candomblé. In case of the latter, the Vodou is just one part, as Candomblé mainly grew out of the enslavement of Yoruba people, just as is the case with Santeria.

Santeria grew out the Yoruba being enslaved by the Spanish Conquistadores upon the island of Cuba, their spirits are known as Orishas, and are different from those found in Vodou. Together with Vodou, Santeria is one of the three separate religious practices found on the island of Cuba, the third being Palo, which has its origins in the Kongo people.

What is interesting with Mexico, is that it is a very Catholic country and lacks the folk religious structure found in Cuba, Haiti, Brazil etc. Instead what we find is individual folk saints that are worked through the established structure of Catholicism, the end result is something more or less similar to the way Catholicism is in Italy, Spain and Portugal. One of the most important aspects of Catholicism—in stark contrast to Protestantism—is the strong veneration of the Virgin Mary, who also tends to be the most common figure of apparition. Knowing this, it of course should not come as a surprise that Mexico's two biggest folk icons are both female, namely Our Lady of Guadalupe and Santa Muerte. Besides the obvious, there is, however, an important difference between the two, for whereas the Virgin of Guadalupe is based upon the apparition of the Virgin Mary (similar to the Portugese Our Lady of Fatima), Santa Muerte is an independent deity. As different as Santa Muerte is, her worship still tends to happen within a Roman Catholic framework, rather than in that of a different faith.

Aside Santa Muerte, one of the most famous figures of death is the Vodou figure of Baron Samedi, and the larger class of spirits known as Gede. It should be noted here, that there is more than just one Baron (besides Samedi, there is Kwimnel, Lakwa and Semtye), though—like all Gede spirits—they all tend to be dandy-like party animals with a strong penchant for being foul-mouthed and sexually driven. Though sometimes Gede spirits are used for practical work, their true association is much more with the realm of death, as they also are connected with the Catholic All Soul's Day, which in Haitian Vodou is known as Fete Gede.

Two figures very similar to Santa Muerte—albeit both male—are the Guatemalan San Pascualito (Rey Pascual) and the Argentinian San La Muerte. Both these deities also appear as grim reapers, yet act outside the area of death, and hence are more associated with health, love and the problems of living. Also being part of Catholic folk faith, they as well are condemned by the Catholic Church, though not to the same degree as is the case with Santa Muerte.

It is also interesting to note that Santa Muerte is certainly not alone in her connection to crime, as another Mexican folk saint is Jesús Malverde. The big different here though, is that he began as a folk hero, as it is said he lived at the end of the 19th century, and was some sort of a Robin Hood type figure. As with Santa Muerte, Jesús Malverde is popular with the poor as well as with drug traffickers.

To many, folk faith may seem as something primitive, yet there is an undeniable beauty in the richness of its symbolism. The major difference with mainstream Christianity, is that folk faith tends to eschew dogmatic metaphysics, and instead focuses more on the reality of ordinary everyday life. The practical nature of folk faith stands in stark contrast to the distance encountered in regular Christianity. The divine is far away and God remains silent; the only consolation given is of his will and plan, as even prayer and devotion does not always work. Folk faith, on the other hand, removes the distance and rather than forcing one to pray for a miracle, offers spiritual intervention through practical workings. As outdated as folk faith may seem, in a world that often seems to be blowing to pieces, it only makes sense for there to be a revival of more practical faiths, which rather than mere consolation offer direct intervention to the many pains and pitfalls of modern day life.

SHORT REVIEWS

AMERICAN HISTORY X:

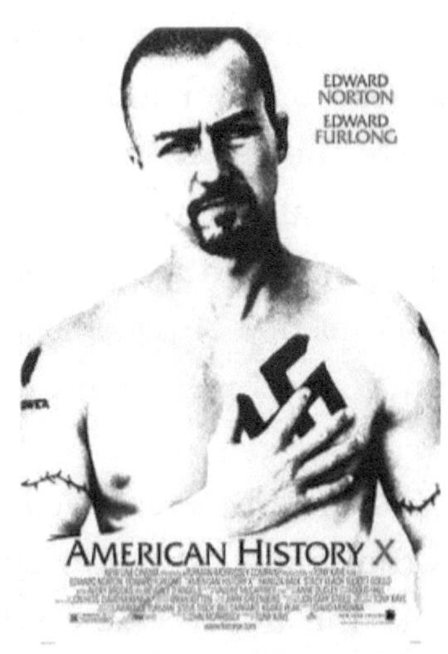

Directed by Tony Kaye, American History X is a stark look into the world of neo-nazism, which after 20 years still feels fresh and actual. The movie is centered around the character of Derek (played by Edward Norton), a young skinhead who is part of an organization intimidating and terrorizing stores run by immigrants and minorities.

The root of Derek's racism lies in his father's low opinion of black people, which is revealed in a flashback of Derek's youth when there is a dinner conversation dominated by the father's dislike for "affirmative action". Derek's father is a fireman who is, more or less, a stereotypical WASP, and though Derek does not originally share his father's inherent racism, he gets turned when his father is killed by a black drug dealer.

Derek becomes a skinhead and quickly rises in the ranks, becoming a figure of great influence. The turning point begins when one night a group of black men try to steal Derek's car, he runs out, shoots at them and then curb stomps one of them. Derek is send to prison for involuntarily manslaughter and immediately becomes accepted by the Aryan Brotherhood. Much to his chagrin, however, he is sent to work in the laundry room where he is paired with a black man called Lamont, with whom he slowly forms a bond.

Eventually Derek runs afoul of the Aryan Brotherhood and is viciously attacked by a number of them. In the hospital ward he is visited by the principal of his younger brother's school, Bob Sweeney, an inspiring black man who seeks to get past the struggles of race and seeks to bring understanding. He informs Derek that his brother is falling down inside that same dark path which has led to his own incarceration. Finally being able to see past all the prejudice, Derek decides to turn his life around and starts to see people for who they are. When eventually he is let out of prison he is fully reformed and determined to guide his brother out of the neo-nazi mindset.

The strength of American History X is that it never dwells long on anything, and instead shows the many elements by which one becomes hooked, as well as the many elements through which one finds redemption. Racism is not inherent in man, but rather comes to possess us through suffering and cultural ignorance. When we surrender to this ignorance and suffering, however, then the only thing we will find in return is the same. The ending of American History X may be disappointing to some, yet serves to make the most crucial point of them all, namely that even when we find redemption, our past always remains and one never knows how it may act upon our future.

AMERICAN HORROR STORY: CULT

Some may of course object to this and write it off as mere sensationalism and sick entertainment, but then it is a horror show, and in that, it is of a serious and visceral quality, so obviously this is not something meant for everyone. The strength of AHS: Cult is that it does not stop at the stereotypical idea of what a cult is but goes all out into the realm of culture and populism, and through its horror paints a picture of how easily it is to become trapped in a mindset.

The central character of AHS: Cult is a young man named Kai Anderson, a quirky young man who enjoys to troll around the internet together with his younger sister Winter. Though originally Kai's exploits are harmless, he quickly comes to be obsessed with power and decides to create a world of his choosing. Kai decides to ride the wave of Populism and loudly cheers when Donald Trump wins the US election, much to the chagrin of his sister who was in favor of Clinton. High on the victory of Trump, Kai wants to become a Populist leader himself and decides to run for the local city council.

What follows is a long series of manipulations and plays of power, in which Kai hooks people into his persona and uses them as pawns in his quest for supremacy. The way Kai hooks and uses people shows the many different facets of Populism and cultish influence. The main hook is always one of helpfulness, Kai sees the distress of the other and wants to offer his help, hence the other is recruited and slowly turned into a pawn.

The way kai further his own political ambitions is through a Trump-like Populism, which he accelerates by deliberately creating an atmosphere of violence and distrust. As he becomes more powerful, however, he becomes more and more obsessed with a cult of personality and seeks to be worshipped as a god. Besides his regular followers, he also amasses a small private army, stereotypical white muscular men with little capacity for thought, and entertains them by telling bedtime stories. The stories of Kai are based upon real-life cults, but he always infuses them with his own persona and twists things around so that they appear as good.

The more powerful Kai gets, all the more paranoid he gets, and the more he tries to manipulate, the more uncertainty he finds. The same is true for his followers, for though his private army shows perfect loyalty through their mindlessness, his original followers are starting to grow weary of Kai, as he has strayed far from his original agenda. But how does one get out? Kai has set everyone up against one another and rules through terror, creating an environment so dangerous, one can no longer even trust one's own self.

Make no mistake about, AHS: Cult is visceral and has a twisted aesthetic, yet it is not mindless entertainment, as through its horror it shows just how dangerous cults (as well as Populism) can be. Despite only being for those into the horror genre, AHS: Cult is a captivating journey through the twisted mind of a cult-leader spiraling out of control and losing every bit of grip upon reality. Its horror may be hard to stomach, but in a naturalist vain, it shows the genuine horror of such events and the darkness of man's mind.

13 REASONS WHY:

Controversy aside, 13 Reasons Why is a powerful look into the world of bullying and its mental impact. More importantly, it is about a kind of bullying that is rather different from its stereotypical form. The bullying that takes place is of a more subtle and emotional nature, and since at moments it almost does not seem to register as bullying, it is easy for it to be neglected.

The story of 13 Reasons Why is centered around high school student Hannah Baker who unable to cope with emotional bullying kills herself, and her story is told through flashbacks as one of her class mates, Clay Jensen, listens to tapes she has left behind detailing the reasons for her suicide. As the series go on, it becomes more and more clear that it is not a traditional form of bullying, but that it is an even more frightening kind of bullying that almost seems to be accepted as regular high school behavior.

It can be said, that perhaps the greatest cruelty is the one appearing as standard behavior and locker room talk, and though what ultimately was the final drop for Hannah was her being raped by the leading school jock, the series for the most part is focused on the smaller instances of casual cruelty. The small things often are what we remember things by, and this counts all the more for our interactions with one another, hence a small word in a moment of anger can have devastating effects. As burdening as the rape is, Hannah's bucket was already filled to the rim because of those many small moments of bullying disguised as ordinary behavior.

The strongest feature of 13 Reasons Why, is that rather than playing a simplistic blame-game, it identifies the many facets that go into not just Hannah's ultimate decision, but also reveals the broken mindsets of those responsible for her death. This is evident with the character of Justin Foley, who was a love interest of Hannah and the subject of the first tape, as he was the first to victimize her. Justin is one of the popular jocks at school, yet upon further revelation is a victim of suffering as well, and similarly it goes for most characters. There is this dynamic of suffering, whereby we are so determined to hide it all away in some magical chest, that we become blind to the suffering we in turn cast upon others.

When it comes to the suffering of others, we are all complicit. It is never good enough to state one did not really do anything, especially since even not being there can make one complicit in such long cycles of trauma. The bullying that leads Hannah to take her own life is rooted in a system of neglect, and an important part of that is a system that often turns a blind eye. School systems, including counselors and psychologists, are often a part of the problem, a view that is clearly expressed in 13 Reasons Why. The final tape of Hannah is not somebody who bullied her, but rather the school psychologist to whom she went after the rape. It is not that the school psychologist did not show kindness, rather it is just that his office was something formal and does not solve or change anything. The distance of everything is a detrimental factor, and we all prefer to wash our hands clean of guilt, something which is especially true for the system, which rather places blame than change its ways.

—Books—

THOMAS SZASZ – THE MYTH OF MENTAL ILLNESS:

Originally published in 1961, Szasz The Myth of Mental Illness remains not just relevant, but in this day and age of Prozac and technology makes an even more interesting read than it did before.

The main point of Szasz is that the very term "mental illness" is a misnomer as it does not involve anything pathogenic. In other words, what is called mental illness is not like the flu, where there is a definite path of the human organism becoming ill. Rather, much too often what is labeled as mental illness is an issue of behavior, and by turning it into illness, we are in turn transforming the person into some disabled someone, since the more we focus on the idea the person is ill, the more we take away from his sense of responsibility.

For Szasz, psychological problems are of the mind and ought to be treated as such, rather than being seen as parts of an actual illness. How would a psychological problem be a disease? To say it is so merely means to rob a person of a true cure, namely by taking away his sense of self-responsibility, which for Szasz is seen as one of the crucial factors in mental well-being, namely one's ability to be responsible for one's own behavior, rather than to seek an escape in the false idea one's mind carries a disease.

PHILIP ZIMBARDO – THE LUCIFER EFFECT:

At moments psychological research shows a degree of cruelty in the way it researches the depths of the human psyche. The most notorious, has to be Harry Harlow's research into social isolation, abandonment and separation, though there is a lot of other research that though much less extreme pushes the boundaries, especially when they use human subjects.

One such case is the Stanford Prison Experiment by Philip Zimbardo, in which a group of human volunteers were placed in the role of either jailer or prisoner. As with the earlier experiments of Stanley Milgram, the aim of Zimbardo was to look into the mechanisms of obedience and authority, and his prison setup was so "successful" that it did not take long before the experiment had to be shut down.

Zimbardo's The Lucifer Effect draws upon the lessons learned from the above experiment, as well as the comparisons of what happened in the Abu Ghraib prison scandal. The message of Zimbardo's work, is that contrary to what we may like to believe, evil deeds are not the work of "bad apples", but rather are allowed through principles of authority.

In the experimental setup of the Stanford Prison Experiment, as well as in the real-life Abu Ghraib prison, the abuse of prisoners was not due to some inherent evil in the perpetrators, but rather it happened because of the situation itself. The point of Zimbardo, is that the responsibility of the

Abu Ghraib scandal does not lie with individuals but with the entire chain of command. There is an entire system in place which allows for the abuse of authority, a lot of which involves the idea of blindness. As in the Milgram Experiments, the abusers were blind to authority and never considered their own moral responsibility. Those in positions of authority, however, were likewise blind to the abuse being perpetrated and hence the abuse only stopped when it came to light outside the immediate chain of command.

We like to believe that perpetrators of gross abuse are somehow deficient, they are however ordinary men and women; as such, the importance of Zimbardo's research is the revelation that the possibility of evil lies inside each one of us. As depressing as this may be, there is also a positive side to it, since for Zimbardo this also means that heroism is within everyone's grasp. To be a hero does not mean one needs something superhuman, rather all it takes is the decision to move past that veil of blindness and ignorance.

Looking past Zimbardo's studies, it is also interesting to see that his work leads to a more general view of man, in which everyone is capable of everything. As such we may argue, that more general occurrences of "evil" are not the product of people radically different from every other regular John or Jane; rather, the possibility of evil always is present in every one of us. The only way to truly defend ourselves, is by recognizing this and always to move towards a cultivation of self-responsibility and a thinking geared towards openness, understanding and integration. Likewise, everyone has it in him to be a hero, it only requires for us to open our eyes and move past the blindness of immediacy.

ROBERT LIFTON – THE PROTEAN SELF:

Most famous for his work on brainwashing and wartime atrocities, Lifton's 1993 The Protean Self, is a celebration of man's capacity for diversity. Proteus is an ancient Greek god of seas and rivers and of fluidity in general, and for Lifton he symbolizes the ability for a person to adapt oneself to what is different from one's own.

Lifton's Protean self serves as an answer to the mental fragility leading towards a self manipulated by a culture of self-sameness. The more open the world becomes, the more one's selfhood comes under attack from alterity, however, rather than being an actual threat, this should be seen as a way to enrichen one's sense of selfhood. Just as once upon a time the self was formed through an identity process of sameness, this open world of multiculturalism, ought to be seen as a framework in which the processes leading towards selfhood become re-actualized.

Rather than weakening the self, the open world leads to an ultimately stronger sense of self, as it is only through fluidity one truly learns to recognize one's own self. Unlike a self caught in "totalism", the Protean self is not afraid to meet the other, as he does not perceive otherness as a threat to his own authenticity. By accepting the other we learn to come to a greater appreciation of selfhood, as we allow for our selfhood to no longer be a product grown out of sameness, rather it stands by its own right, in a landscape of diversity.

CULTS, CULTURE & FREEDOM
by Steven Van Neste

-1- Rousseau famously begins his "The Social Contract" by stating that man, though born free, is everywhere in chains. Perhaps to most, such reason is no longer of today's order, at least not in the western first world; yet that we take freedom for granted, reveals the perilous nature of first world society. Granted, Ronald Reagan famously declared freedom is always one generation away from eradication, the majority of people can never fathom anything outside their freedom. But then, of course, what is freedom? One of the problems, is that we tend to associate the world almost exclusively with politics, and hence, more often than not, the word is almost synonymous with democracy. Of course, even this does not clear anything, since what is meant by democracy is usually rather vague, and indeed, totalitarian regimes often call themselves democratic as well.

-2- The idea of political freedom is not what we are after here (at least not directly), nor are we interested in the notion of freedom as a metaphysical term, rather, what this work seeks to delve into, is the notion of freedom from a more or less socio-psychological point of view. Rousseau's declaration of everywhere man being found in chains was relative to the society in which he lived. The scenario is of course different today, yet still everywhere man is found in chains, and this regardless of the political freedom that has since been gained. The first thing that must be understood here, is that it is impossible to be perfectly free from those chains. To live always implies a certain amount of bondage, hence it debatable if one is born free, since every step of the way we are faced with decisions, and though we may be free in what we decide, we always are chained to the fact we must decide.

-3-   Let us first, then, imagine a Robinson Crusoe type setting. At first it may seem like one would enjoy perfect freedom, yet this is not so. Even stranded on a desert island we are bound by certain chains, since even at the most minimal level, we are never free from our corporeal situation. We are never free from our biological functions, nor are we ever free from the natural elements, hence we are always bound by the fact there are certain necessities we must obey simply in order to live. We cannot live outside certain basic parameters, as they are what defines our living. When the pains of hunger strike us, we are forced to eat. Granted, one could naively argue we are free to choose not to eat, however, this is a misnomer; as it is an argument belonging to freedom as an abstract concept, rather than as a human something. A person must find nourishment in order to live, hence this need binds us and restricts us, since if we were to deny nourishment then our life would end.

-4-   A Robinson Crusoe type freedom might seem enticing, as the only thing that binds one is the immediacy of our biological needs, however, there is always more to man than simply this. No one is an island on his own, and for the most part, man enjoys certain social interaction. As such, what we find on a desert island is not so much freedom, but rather isolation. The fact always remains, that we are never born as isolated creatures, but always are born as part of a system. More importantly, social interaction and feelings of "warmth" are essential to proper development. It is not just biological needs that must be met, in order for a new born to be able to properly develop, but there are social needs as well. We are born helpless, rather than free, and hence our lives are, from early on, defined through bondage.

-5-   Perhaps it is because of man's innate helplessness, that he is so driven by the concept of freedom. With this in mind, it is also interesting to note the evolution of religious thought; specifically, the movement from primitive religious thought (arising out of the functional needs of agricultural society), towards legislative religious thought (arising out of a need to codify society), and then finally turning into metaphysical religion. Especially this last transformation is of great interest, as it seeks to fully break outside of time. The movement whereby religion becomes metaphysical, is through a process of separation, which gives rise to the concepts of temporality and eternity. Helplessness appears antithetical to freedom, as it means we always are enslaved to something, hence, what is desired is a movement away from this, and it is precisely this desire which fuels metaphysics.

-6-   The central theme of metaphysical religion is the need for finalization, hence the importance of eschatology. The oddity in man, is that though we fear the eternal, we crave it as well, hence, what we desire above all is a frozen eternity. We are not only born helpless and in shackles, we also are always a victim of the ravages of time. Eternity weighs us down every step of the way, and the only way to counter this, is by creating a different kind of eternity, one in which we may be free.

-7-			Though culture may appear as different from religion, the two are not just closely related, but it may even be argued culture grew out of religion. The culture surrounding holidays is an important illustration here, since they always grew out of religious observation, and both the words 'holiday' and 'feast' are derived from the idea of something sacred. Originally holidays were meant to mark cyclical events, and hence belonged to the realm of eternal recurrence. As religion turned metaphysical, however, the idea of the holiday came to be more of something marking the promise of salvation.

-8-			The first thing that ought to be understood, when looking at the connection between culture and religion, is that the word 'culture' is derived from the Latin 'cultura', which in turn is derived from 'cultus'; the meaning of which is both cultivation and worship. Culture was born out of the religiosity of early society, and just as religion transformed, so did culture, hence, as religion turned metaphysical, culture did as well.

-9-			As mentioned above, one of the main features of metaphysical religion is its need for finalization. It is not just that man, by nature, seeks meaning, he also wants this meaning to be binding. In short, we do not just want our meaning to be for us, but for it to bind the other as well. The evolution of society, is not just determined through individual populations, but rather through the way different populations interact with one another. It is not just that, as with Thomas Hobbes, there is a society of each man against every other, as there also is the reality of each society against every other. The reason why history is tainted by religious wars, is not so much because of religion, but rather because of man's innate desire for homogeneity. Man is a creature of habit, so much so, that even chaos has been turned into something lawful, as we demand for there to be a reality transcending both chance and habit. Hence, the idea of culture, taken by itself, is nothing but religion stripped of some of its outer clothing.

-10-   A thought frequently found with those denying Evolution is that one never encounters a half-species, this however, says more about the way our mind works, than it says anything about Evolution. Our mind is always biased towards totality, hence, everything we perceive is always felt as being a complete picture. Even more so, when we look at the world, we never perceive any edges, vision always seems to continue beyond its scope. When we look at a landscape, we don't see the landscape as ending at the edge of our vision; this is true even of people who suffer from Neglect Syndrome, in spite of missing part of their perception, everything still feels complete. Completion is the ever-present bias in our perception, and hence it should come as no surprise that it also dominates the way we think. The reason why some vehemently oppose Evolution, is not just because they adhere to Creationism, but also because more generally, we like everything to just be. The notion of becoming is a frightful idea, hence we are always drawn towards being.

-11- The etymology of 'society' is not just one of unity and companionship, but also of following. Unity can only exist when there is something followed, hence, society always goes together with the idea of law. For society to work, however, this idea of following must be complete and thus at every step, society always entails the surrender of the individual. Enlightenment philosophers such as Locke and Rousseau may appear rather different from the authoritarianism of Hobbes, yet in all of them is an element of bondage. Going back to Rousseau's opening statement, what is rather the case, is that everywhere we obsess over freedom, yet always are in chains. This, of course, is only to be expected, as even Anarchistic models require certain voluntary surrender, yet it also comes to show just how complicated the matter truly is.

-12- As mentioned, our mind is always geared towards totality, hence, society always appears as something totalizing. Society must be absolutely binding, as is the culture through which society operates. One may object here, pointing out the many radical changes that have occurred in society. Great revolutions have altered society a great deal, yet this does not at all change the point that society by itself is totalizing. For the longest time, Absolutism was the norm, then came the Enlightenment, which gave rise to Liberal Democracy. It may be true that Enlightenment thinkers did not take Absolutism as a final product, yet they still envisioned a totalizing society, as such Liberal Democracy became the new Absolutism.

-13-			Our thinking always points towards something finished and absolute. Marx' Dialectical Materialism might have been open to seeing society as an evolving something, yet it still projected there being an end-goal, society as a finished product. Thinkers attempting to create a new society, always do so with this in mind, namely, that this new society will be the absolute. Nobody ever wants to create a stepping stone, but always wants a finished product. As such, there really is no wonder to the saying that history is written by the winner, as a dominant society will always see its transgressions as necessary steps.

-14-			Rather than freedom, what we desire above all is cessation of worry and helplessness. This is true not just in social matters, but even in religious ones as well. Man's need for an afterlife is not just because we fear the ending of life, but also because we desire the satisfaction of being at peace; the afterlife, as such, is a world where we can be free from any kind of worry. Of course, the promise of peace never takes away the pangs of life, and thus it does not take much for life to become something lived solely in order to reach the after-life. Here it is also important to note, that this mechanism is not at all restricted to religious thought within the Judea-Christian tradition, but is also a standard in Eastern thought and its many present day New Age incarnations.

-15- Culture, originally speaking, can be said to be the atmosphere necessary for religious fulfillment. As mentioned already, the idea of holidays is important here, and where many originally were tied to agriculture, as religion became metaphysical, holidays turned into a series of events, goading us to the idea of promise and afterlife. This remains true, even when society becomes more secular, hence why in the West Christmas remains important, and has been turned into a Holiday period, together with the arrival of the new year.

16- Culture may be described as the overall feeling of a society. As such, what we generally fear in clashes with different societies, is not so much acts, but rather alien sentiment. Today's society is one marked by a remarkable level of global openness, yet the more open society becomes, the greater is the danger of cultural hostility. The current trend of so-called 'religious liberty' is a desperate attempt by the culturally ignorant, to force both closed-ness and devolution. Likewise, the anti-Islamic wave of Populism, is not so much rooted in religious dogma, as it is a result of associated culture.

-17- Guy Debord once described how culture is centered around the search for lost unity. In today's landscape of Populism this seems to be all the more accurate, for not only is the other seen as someone trying to disrupt our own culture, but Populism also states that our culture has been disrupted already through progressive politics. The Populist demands for there to be unity, which in turn leads to the fulfillment of the promise, namely a homogenous society that is self-enclosed and runs like some sort of socio-political perpetuum mobile.

-18-   The irony with this current wave of right-wing Populism, is that essentially it is Marxist in nature. The essence of a Marxist society is a society in which there is no other and hence no apparent struggle. The Marxist utopia knows no struggle because everything is given and there is no longer the possibility of the contrary. The idea behind the Populist state is a perfect uniformity of culture and an organization which accounts for everything. The wall so desired by Trump is not just because he desires to keep out foreigners, but more importantly, it is symbolic of his desire to have an America in which everything is self-same. Here, it also ought to be noted that the Populist stance against Progressivism is not to be seen as being against "the worker", to the contrary, the Populist ideology generally thrives by promising the return of jobs.

-19-   The freedom cherished by the Populist is cultish in nature, as it seeks to establish freedom solely within the confines of a dominant culture. In essence, it may be said, that the cultish idea of freedom is one devoid of choice, since it is established that in one's freedom one shall always do what is "right and proper", or in other words: what is demanded.

-20-   It is easy for culture to become a trap, as it does not take much for society itself to become a cult. Hitler, Stalin, Mao, Putin, Trump; all these names are behind a movement which seeks to turn the whole of society into something cult-like, as all of them are leaders forcing an identity upon the society over which they rule. Beyond these examples of obvious totalitarianism, it also exists in more moderate forms, something that becomes evident whenever a nation speaks of values as being of their nation, so American values, British values, Belgian values etc. The problem here, is that whenever we conceive of a value in such a way, then we automatically come to demean it. The philosopher Immanuel Kant was on the right track here with his notion of the categorical imperative, which attempts to trace morality to universality. Kant's theory may be a little too metaphysically driven, yet it still leads to a valid point, namely that we should always consider the universal rather than the immediate.

-21-   It is one of the true quirks of man, that always is he readier to fight for freedom than to contemplate it. Looking at history, it becomes clear that more than anything our notion of freedom is rather selective, as it means to be obedient to a certain identity. The mistake we make, as such, is that whenever we think of freedom we only consider it within the narrow corridor of our cultural identity and fail to realize the broader concept of freedom on a universal scale.

22-   The love we have for freedom, generally, always comes together with a disgust for freedom in a more universal sense; or perhaps to put it in a better way: our love for freedom goes hand in hand with our fear of it. What we desire, as such, is a carefully programmed simulation. Real freedom is unworkable, as it also means I have to allow for the freedom of the other, hence we come to a new interpretation of freedom, in which freedom is only valid for those partaking in a society of self-sameness. This need for self-sameness often goes so far, that the other becomes dehumanized. This was evidenced in ancient societies, for instance in the Greek world, only the male Greek was seen as properly being human, whereas foreigners were considered barbarian.

-23-		As much as we may now pretend to be modern, our mindset still is more or less the same as it was in ancient times. Even more so, the more "modern" we become, the more we become trapped in a teleological anthropology. As modern man, we live under the delusion that everything must necessarily point to our being-now, in other words, who we are now is the fulfillment of what it means to be human, and everything that remains other, is considered less human. The western first world, as a whole, is very similar to the world of ancient Roman citizenry, in that we only allow the other his freedom in as much as he conforms to the western paradigm.

-24-		What always happens though, is that whenever a society intends to reel in the other, it also becomes more open to the influence of the other. To convert the other, we have to use his own terms, as integration always means we must go into a zone where self and other come to overlap. Through our desire to convert the other, we come to the idea of meeting the other halfway, and this is how both society and our sense of self come to evolve. In spite of any humanistic delusions, Globalism is a necessary factor in societal evolution, which is why it is such a threat to the Populist.

-25-   As mentioned early on, no one is an island on his own, as man has a general tendency to social stimulation, and this precisely is what complicates the complex of the other, as he presents himself as both friend and enemy. No matter how much we are drawn to self-sameness, we always are in need of the other. Even those who wish to retreat from the world in a drive of self-obsession, they still betray a desperation for the other, as their sense of self is derived from the Vedantic principle of "neti, neti", which means "not that, not that". Similarly, the Populist and the racist, no matter how much they hate the other, have an insatiable need for the other, since without the other they cannot ever further their agenda.

-26-   As much as Trump likes to rage against immigrants, and people of different faiths and lifestyles; the only reason such a platform of ignorance has led to his sad victory, is because of the importance of the other; after all, what would a white nationalist be without the presence of what is other than white? The success of Populism always depends on the reality of the other, without which there is nothing to bind things together. This is seen in fundamentalist religion as well, which always pits the believer against the sinner, or the light against the dark, God against the Devil etc. Trump did not win the US presidential election on the merit of his own self, but solely upon the backs of the many others he seeks to demonize; similarly, ISIS became influential not by their own strength, but solely through the presence of the other.

-27-			Whether it is religious or political, fundamentalism can only thrive when there is the presence of the other, which is why in Orwell's Nineteen Eighty-Four, there is the need for a perpetual war against otherness. Though Nineteen Eighty-Four mainly is centered on the theme of constant governmental supervision and the—almost—absolute lack of privacy; it also shows a world of such total fundamentalism, that the world is divided strictly along the lines of otherness. The different nations in Nineteen Eighty-Four exist no longer because of any perceived values, but solely as structures of what may be dubbed "self-same-otherness". In the world of Winston Smith, there is no longer anything that binds society, hence his reality is an entire void based upon the promise that one day the other nation will be conquered. The fundamentalism is so deep, that it is not even known what the other is, and at moments the name of the other even changes.

-28-			One of the mottos used by Orwell in his Nineteen Eighty-Four is: "war is peace", an idea which perfectly sums up the agenda of Populism, fundamentalism etc. The agenda of the Populist always presents itself as something positive, as something that will bring peace and prosperity, as something that will it all great again; yet in reality it can only survive through a constant war mongering. It is interesting, as such, that when it comes to western Populism the public enemy number one is the Islamic religion. The irony here is that it makes for an almost perfect Nineteen Eighty-Four setup, especially since one of the main principles—against which the Populist is very much on guard—is that of Jihad, which translates to "struggle ", and which in the hands of Islamic fundamentalism means the eternal struggle against otherness, just in the same way as western Populism imagines there ought to be an eternal struggle against what is other.

-29-				Even when we look at stereotypical cults such as The Peoples Temple and Branch Davidians, what we find is a structure that cannot exist without the presence of the other. As much as these cults removed themselves from regular society, they always remained dependent upon it. Jim Jones may have gone to such an extreme as to remove almost his entire following to the jungles of Guyana, yet the USA always remained with him. A cult cannot ever free itself from the society it seeks to detach itself from. Even more so, the society so hated by the cult is detrimental not just to its agenda, but more importantly to its methods of recruitment.

-30-				In certain parts of eastern thought, there is a deliberate movement away from the material world which is seen as false, as reality lies in a realm of non-materialism, which consequently is where freedom is to be found. It must be admitted that there is a valid point to this, as freedom cannot ever be truly achieved due to the limitations of material reality. Be as this may, however, to turn freedom into a metaphysical concept achieves nothing, as it remains dependent upon the material. Even more so, freedom in such a metaphysical sense is entirely without meaning, as it is devoid of any bearing whatsoever. As interesting as it may be to contemplate freedom in a deeper sense, it is at the end a play of smoke and mirrors, something akin to imagining a white dot upon a white background.

-31-	Perhaps we may state that freedom is only relevant in a world of chains, and hence what gives freedom its meaning is what we do with these chains. As such, we should not let freedom be defined by our own culture, but rather we should attempt to create a culture based upon a more open-minded and positive conception of freedom. The presence of the other should not be seen as a threat, but rather as an opportunity to enrichen the experience of one's own selfhood.

-32-	In spite of its tough sounding rhetoric, Populism is always governed by fear, and as such its call upon a perceived superior culture is in reality one of enslavement. The great America promised by Trump is in reality nothing but a backwards nation afraid of its own shadow. Societal evolution cannot ever be stopped, and hence Populism achieves nothing but a furthering of ignorance. What is done is done and hence there can never be an "again", for all that comes to be is always new. Looking at past culture and wishing to bring it back, is akin to Homo Sapiens wishing to become Homo Erectus again.

-33-	Freedom is envisioned as something grand and precious, and indeed it ought to be treated as such, which is why—in line with Kant's categorical imperative—we would do well to always approach freedom from a more or less universal point of view, rather than from within a framework of a narrow-minded culture. Societal cohesion is achieved not through discrimination, but rather through inclusion. As pointed out by Amy Chua in her "Day of Empire", the greatness of empires always goes together with a measure of inclusion, whereas intolerance quickly leads to decline. Societal evolution operates much in the same way as species evolve (hence why there is no turning back); diversity leads to strength, as it gives much greater elbow room when it comes to adaptability.

-34-   We may be born helpless in a dog eat dog world, yet this certainly does not mean we ought to live life this way. The barbarity of bare life may appear to turn human existence into a bleak something, yet even Hobbes thought essentially man desires security. Renaissance philosophers such as Hobbes, Jean Bodin and Hugo Grotius often are seen as figures promoting autocratic rule, yet in reality they were far ahead of their time, since their ideas of strict law were also opposed to theocracy.

-35-   If one wishes to truly cherish freedom, then rather than barricading himself behind a Trumpian wall, one should open oneself towards the presence of the other. How can we ever feel secure if we always have the specter of the ominous other ready to take it all away? The great sadness of many societies has always been their restriction of freedom to a certain class of people, yet in reality all this achieves is to reinforce the bare life reality it so desperately seeks to escape. Tolerance not only is beneficial to having a varied pool of social "genetics", it also is beneficial when it comes to the more personal evolution of the self. Who we are is not some fixed narrative, but rather our self exists as something that can either grow towards a more multifaceted something, or remain in the mire. We should not allow for the concepts of self and freedom to become reduced to either cultural or metaphysical oddities, rather we should allow for them to become all embracing. The other is not an obstacle towards the self's authenticity, but rather is what allows for said authenticity to be genuine. It is easy to feel sure about oneself when surrounded by people of a self-same vision, but a whole lot harder to feel sure about oneself in a landscape of alterity. The boisterous rhetoric of Trumpian Populists, as such, betrays a self too weak to stand upon its own legs. Similarly, the baker unable to bake a gay wedding cake, or county clerk unable to wed a gay couple, are people betraying a rather weak sense of selfhood. The presence of the other ought to be treated as a gift rather than a burden, as it is the other who allows for the cultivation of the self. If the idea of a gay marriage threatens one's straight marriage, then what does this not say about said straight marriage? Whenever the strength of one's conviction requires the deafening applause of a peer-group structure, then whatever one may talk about has little to do with freedom, as any kind of such self-exaltation is always fraudulent. Genuine self-authenticity is what stands by its own right in a landscape of alterity. To make a play upon Kant's categorical imperative; I ought to constitute my selfhood as such that it may stand in a landscape of universal alterity. The color of one's skin or one's sexual orientation should never communicate anything extra; where the story of the self lies, is always in the way we meet and treat the other, and the only way we can ever bring honor to our own self, lies in our ability to meet the other.

NOTES ON CRITICAL THINKING

When it comes to preventing ourselves from being hoodwinked, nothing is more important than to cultivate critical thinking skills, yet the oddity is that both terms ("critical" and "thinking") are complicated enough on their own, that when appearing together we generally have no idea as to what is meant.

As such, the first thing that ought to be understood, is that "critical thinking" has no direct connection to what is known as "critical theory", for whereas the latter is concerned with a (more or less) Marxist approach to modern day society and culture, the latter belongs exclusively to the domain of epistemology.

Critical thinking is a thinking that is concerned with thought itself, as such it ties in with the field of logic, though whereas logic is of a more mathematical nature, critical thinking tends to be more concerned with human nature.

The error often made, is that critical thinking is a philosophical enterprise. True enough, critical thinking grew out of philosophical enterprise, but then so did a lot of things, including physics, and most physicists probably prefer not to be lumped in with philosophy.

Another common error is that critical thinking means a selling out to science, that we thus believe everything science says is always automatically correct. This definitely is not the case, since science itself is built upon principles of critical thinking, rather than it being the other way. It is the scientific method that led to science, not the other way around!

Perhaps the most common reason people fear critical thinking is because it is falsely imagined it is naturally opposed to anything religious or spiritual, this however is not so. In fact, the famous principle known as Ockham's Razor (calling upon us to disregard anything not necessary), is named after the Christian monk William of Ockham, who in spite of his faith was deeply into the cultivation of proper thinking.

The reason critical thinking stands outside science and philosophy, is because it is not so much concerned with content (at least not in the direct sense) as rather it is concerned with thinking itself. Here it must be understood though, that thinking is not at all concerned with the concept of thinking in a more metaphysical sense.

So what thinking are we concerned with then? To some this may seem as a headache already, since there is thinking and there is thinking and there is etc. It is true, the concept of thinking can easily be turned into something torturous, but this is not the scope of critical thinking. So, rest assured, Heidegger's "What is called Thinking?" has nothing to do with any of this, so you may sleep soundly in the knowledge critical thinking is not some word salad thing.

A sound night's sleep is (probably) more precious than

anything else. Yet what is thinking? One wakes up refreshed and yet still is none the wiser. What is thinking? Many have gone on tangents concerning this topic, yet in reality we all know what is meant by the word: it is a processing of information in order to make sense of things.

So why does it need to be critical? This probably is where it gets a little odd. If thinking is just what we all know as thinking, then doesn't that mean there's also no right and wrong to it? Indeed, thinking has no moral bearing and there absolutely is no difference between trying to differentiate between McDonalds and Burger King as there is between good and evil.

If thinking is this simple, then how could there be critical thinking? Well simply put, critical thinking merely says that if we want to maximize our thinking, then we ought to be in maximum control of the flow of information. Thinking always favors totality, as such we want to be in possession of all the information. Suppression of information might be common in the way groups seek to control thinking, but for sure it does not bear upon the nature of thinking itself.

So to end, what is critical thinking; well, it is that moving outside what is programmed. To be critical means one can compare similar lines of thought and see for oneself what makes the most sense. In a deeper sense, what this means is that thinking is not a project that can ever be finished. At every moment of our lives, there is a constant flow of information; to think critically means we always understand there is more and thus we always are driven to think more.

ABOUT THE COVER ART

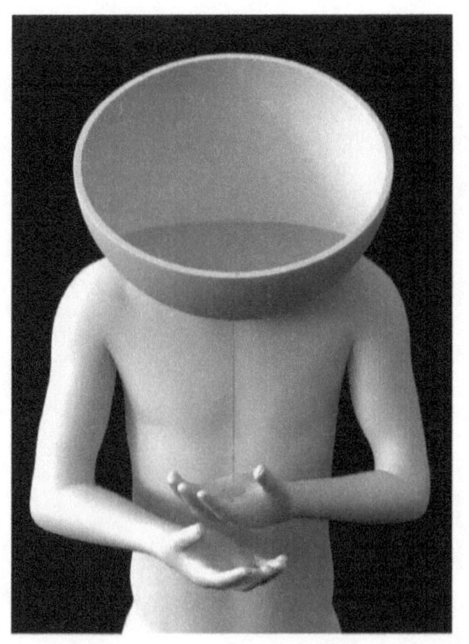

The art for the cover was kindly provided to us by Kyuin Shim, a South Korean artist specializing in sculpture and digital art. His work concerns alterations and distortions of the human body, as well as a theme of fluidity.

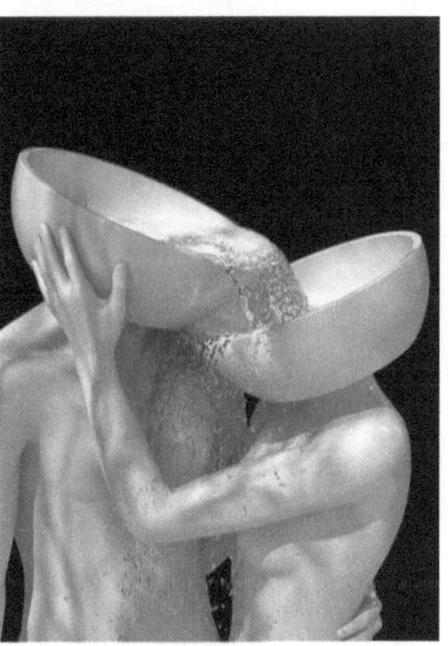

For more information:
http://magshim.cafe24.com/wp/
https://society6.com/shimkyuin
https://www.behance.net/shimkyuin

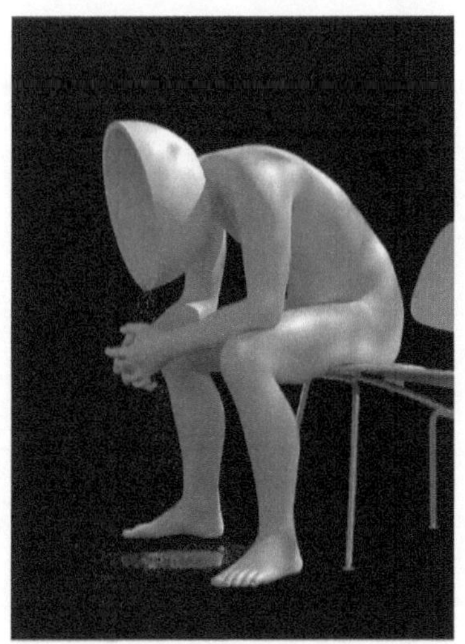

NIHILOCRACY
book 1: Nomos
Steven Van Neste

INTRODUCTION TO LOGIC
AND TO THE METHODOLOGY OF DEDUCTIVE SCIENCES
Alfred Tarski

Kathleen Taylor
BRAIN WASHING
The science of thought control
NOW WITH NEW PREFACE
OXFORD LANDMARK SCIENCE

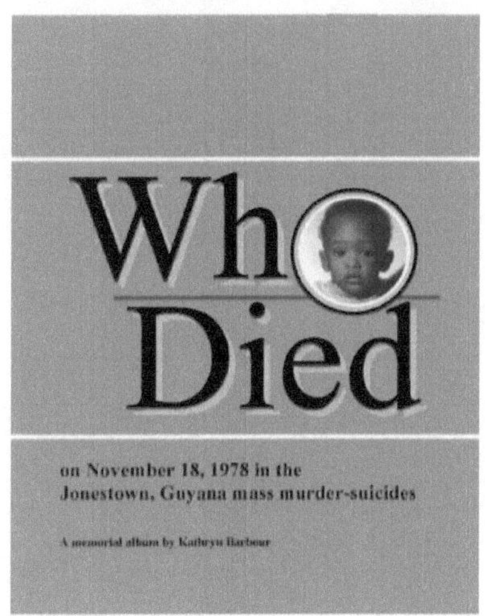

Who Died
on November 18, 1978 in the Jonestown, Guyana mass murder-suicides
A memorial album by Kathryn Barbour

LAURA JOHNSTON KOHL
JONESTOWN SURVIVOR
AN INSIDER'S LOOK
IN MEMORY OF THE VICTIMS OF THE JONESTOWN TRAGEDY
NOV. 18, 1978
JONESTOWN, GUYANA

PENGUIN CLASSICS
CLAUDE LÉVI-STRAUSS
Tristes Tropiques

THE SERPENT AND THE RAINBOW
A HARVARD SCIENTIST'S ASTONISHING JOURNEY INTO THE SECRET SOCIETIES OF HAITIAN VOODOO, ZOMBIS, AND MAGIC
WADE DAVIS

DAY OF EMPIRE
How Hyperpowers Rise to Global Dominance—and Why They Fall
AMY CHUA

www.ingramcontent.com/pod-product-compliance
Lightning Source LLC
Chambersburg PA
CBHW031316250726
48656CB00005B/1829